**D
Those who**

Lived by Truth

Died for Truth

Loved but Truth

Spread just Truth

Satyameva Jayathe
<Truth Alone Triumphs>

Math Kids Book I - The Tiger's Nest

faster and simpler math: multiplication

Payal Roy &

Kaustava Roy

Contents

Acknowledgements
Preface
Prologue

Chapter 1 Things that go bop! *Learning to multiply up to fives*
1.1 What is multiplication?
1.2 Commutation
1.3 Association
1.4 A multiplication table
1.5 Tables from 1 to 5

Chapter 2 Horror on Halloween! *Learning to multiply up to ten*
2.1 The 5 x 10 table
2.2 Distribution
2.3 10s times trick
2.4 Using partners
2.5 Tables from 6 to 10

Chapter 3 The Witch plans a return. *Learning to add a simple series*
3.1 Rearrange addition to do multiplication
3.2 Use the 5x5 table to add a number series
3.3 Use the 5x6 table to add a series
3.4 General formula to add a series
3.5 Find the Nth number of a series

Chapter 4 The butterfly effect. *Learning to multiply up to twenty*
4.1 Multiplying numbers between 10 and 20
4.2 Quick method
4.3 11s times trick
4.4 Quick method extended

Chapter 5 Friends unite. *Learning to multiply up to 100 & do simple permutations and combinations*
5.1 Calculate simple combinations

5.2 Factorials and Permutations
5.3 Multiplying 2-digit numbers
5.4 Quick methods
5.5 Difference of squares method

Chapter 6 Flight to destiny. *General multiplication, multiples, factors and divisibility*
6.1 General multiplication
6.2 The 2-line method
6.3 Introducing negative numbers
6.4 Modified 2-line method
6.5 Multiples, factors and divisibility

Chapter 7 Friend or foe. *Multiplication to find areas of shapes*
7.1 Areas of squares, rectangles, and triangles
7.2 Areas of polygons and circles
7.3 Maximum area & minimum perimeter
7.4 Petalgons and stretched shapes
7.5 Areas using average length

Chapter 8 The mind stone's owner. *Multiplication to find volumes of shapes*
8.1 Volumes of prisms and cylinders
8.2 Summing squares series
8.3 Volumes of pyramids and cones
8.4 Volumes of spheres and hemispheres

Chapter 9 The Tiger's Nest. *Multiplication with different number systems*

Acknowledgements

This book has been possible through loving help from many people. It is inspired from a wish to create a math book that teaches faster and simpler math techniques through the form of an adventure story that extolls good virtues. The authors have been fortunate to know excellent earlier works in math such as Vedic Mathematics by Swami Bharati Krishna Tirtha, and Life of Fred by Stanley Fredric Schmidt. These two texts, especially the former, have strongly influenced the authors.

We want to thank our brave and kind editor, Brian Tibbetts, for taking on the challenge of editing a manuscript from novice writers in a near-nascent genre. His efforts are responsible for making the book a much more intelligible and enjoyable reading.

We want to thank our families (especially Upasana Roy and also Ina Roy and Shobhan Majumdar) for their continual feedback during the early stages of the work.

We want to thank our friendly neighborhood English professor, Scott Dionne, for his advice regarding writing and publishing.

We can't forget to thank three boys who really love math – Muni, Rishi and Sunny – for keeping it a kid- acceptable book and helping with the cover page.

Finally, the authors would like to express their eternal gratitude to their parents (Dr. Arati Roy & Prof Kunal Roy, and Mrs. Rekha Majumdar & Mr. Sushil K. Majumdar) for instilling in them a love toward math and toward noble qualities.

© 2017 by Payal & Kaustava Roy.
Cover Picture: courtesy www.pexels.com

Preface

We learn by observing patterns. For example, a pattern that we have observed is that fruits only fall down from trees; they do not fall up. They also fall faster from the higher branches.

We have seen that the height they drop from is proportional to the square of the time it takes for them to hit the ground. In fact, we have found this relationship to be true for all objects, not just fruits.

Mathematics is the best language for expressing and relating such physical patterns to uncover knowledge. Using it, we can capture knowledge about falling objects in a mathematical equation. This equation can help deduce or predict other things. It can tell us that if a ball takes 4 seconds to fall to the bottom of a well, then the well is about 80 meters deep!

We can gain socio-economic knowledge through math as well. We might see that a democracy's strength is proportional to the education of its population.

In this educational novel, the student will learn to see multiplicative patterns and ways to simplify them to solve various problems. Pattern recognition skills, concentration, and memory will grow along with the student's ability to multiply—faster than a calculator in many cases!

The book has two sections. Section-I, for five to seven year olds, contains the first three chapters, and is in a fun Dr. Seussy style. Section-II, for seven to twelve year olds, covers the rest of the book's nine chapters.

Younger readers might need help from older siblings or grown-ups to understand this book. However, learning math could make for a good opportunity to spend quality family time together. Please share what you liked and did not like about the book with us, so we can improve it further.

Education must also be about building character. A patient, optimistic, and bold person will live a richer life un-crippled by stress and anxiety. A noble person will do good work for the world.

The authors believe one needs both secular and spiritual knowledge to develop a complete personality. The fields of both science and religion have had their share of fraud and misrepresentation. However, they also have many good things to offer. Using the power of logic (with help from Math), one can sift out and use what is beneficial for humanity.

If you want to serve truly in any field, including mathematics, you need a noble character. Only then will your knowledge serve humanity properly. The young heroes of this book are fearless, optimistic, patient, and noble. We hope the reader will want to be like them and thus bring little pieces of heaven to earth.

Please note that in this book, God is referred to as "She." This is to honor the ancient tradition of God as Mother where She is revered higher than as Father, for love and mercy are higher than law and punishment.

Happy reading!

Prologue

"Enough delay! Hand me the mind stone, kids, and you won't get hurt," Teninone said. The Demon King had been desperately seeking the mind stone for years. With it, he could bend minds to his will.

The four kids stood quietly in Teninone's Royal Hall; unafraid, though surrounded by demon soldiers.

Teninone surveyed the kids' faces to see which one would be most likely to talk. It could be the little girl, Matya, with the funny eyes; or maybe the older girl, Maya, who seemed persuadable. Could it be the older boy, Pratham, their spokesperson? But it was the younger boy, Thulo, who spoke up first.

"Telephone, you don't scare us! You don't deserve the mind stone and you will never get it," Thulo said. This was definitely not what the Demon King wanted to hear.

General Greymon hissed at Thulo, "Say our leader's name with respect. He is Lord Teninone."

Thulo retorted, "He is unworthy of any title. In fact, he should be called the Brainless Gnome."

Teninone seethed. "Impudent kid. You don't know my power! Do you know what Teninone means? It means Ten-in-one! I have ten clones. We see, think, and do ten things at once—"

"And make ten times the mess," ten-year-old Pratham now added calmly. Then, turning to the soldiers, he said, "Evil always has an end, and your ruler's end is near. Leave him now and save yourselves."

Teninone was enraged but knew that if he killed the kids he might never find the mind stone. The mind stone was visible only to its owner and to whomever it was passed.

Ignoring the boys, he addressed Maya, "There is a prophecy that my death will neither be at the hand of demons, demigods, man, nor beast; neither by disease nor by one that is either young or old. I am practically immortal! As long as I live, I can do great things for the world with the mind stone. Tell me where the mind stone is and your family and friends will receive protection under my rule."

"If you promise not to misuse its power and also let humans and demons coexist peacefully, I will give it to you. I do not want a war where many innocent people—both humans and demons will die," Maya said. Teninone nodded his assent. With the mind stone, he might not need a war to become the ruler of the world.

Pratham and Thulo protested loudly, "You can't trust him! Don't give him the stone Maya!" But Maya had already started walking towards Teninone, a glowing crystal in her hand.

SECTION – I

Chapter 1 Things that go bop!

Learning to multiply up to fives

Topics *1.1 What is multiplication?, 1.2 Commutation, 1.3 Association, 1.4 A multiplication table, 1.5 Tables from 1 to 5*

1.1 What is multiplication?

It was a cold, cold December. However, in his living room, Pratham was warm and cozy this winter. It was eight o'clock, not yet time for bed; so he sat at the piano to practice instead. Just then, to his surprise— Bop! Bop! Two blows landed on his head. This could only be Thulo. But where had he fled?

Mom was on the sofa grading test papers. This time, her students had done much better. Mom smiled happily sipping her chai, when two bops landed on her head, making her papers fly. Chai spilled on her papers and on her pretty dress. Before she could catch him, Thulo had escaped.

Dad was writing at the side table. Thulo climbed onto Dad's shoulders and pulled off his cap. He threw it afar and began to laugh. Bop! Bop! Two bops landed on Dad's head and the culprit's eyes twinkled like stars as he fled.

Yes—Thulo. The nickname meant "soft as cotton." As a baby, Thulo's hands were indeed soft as cotton. But in six short years his hands had grown strong; he could run very fast; and bop quite hard.

"Mom, Thulo bopped me again!" ten-year-old Pratham complained as he rubbed his head.

"Say something. Discipline your son." Mom looked angrily at Dad. "This is not the way to have some fun. Wasn't he supposed to teach you math right now? He should be doing that instead of running around."

Ever since a curse had made Dad forget math the boys were sad. "Don't feel sad, you can teach math to Dad," their Mom had told them. That had cheered them up. If they could teach math to Dad, may be the curse was not so bad.

Dad looked at Thulo, "No more bopping, Thulo, my dear. This hit-and-run game isn't nice, you hear? You can't just bop people out of the blue. What if others did this to you?"

"Okay", said Thulo with an innocent smile, that seemed to say "Okay for now. You'll forget in a while."

Two days before Thulo had learnt a new song from school. So close to his heart, he loved its tune:

> Little Bunny Foo Foo
> Hopping through the forest
> Scoopin' up the field mice
> Bopping em on the head!
> ...

He enjoyed singing, and this song was so fun. However, he didn't care about the part when Bunny Foo Foo was warned.

That day, coming home, and happily singing this song, he started bopping people's heads to everyone's alarm. Pretty soon he found people running from his song; so he sang in his head to keep bopping along.

"But, Dad" Thulo protested, with an angelic face, "I was only teaching you how to multiply in your head."

"So teach multiplication in his head. Not on ours," Pratham complained.

"Multiplication, did you say?" asked his Dad. "Is this what you'll teach me today, my lad?"

"Yup - I'll show you how to times (multiply) two numbers with me. Just add the same number many times, mentally. I bopped 2 + 2 + 2 times. I bopped six times. Adding two three times gives six. We say: 2 times 3 is 6, okay? And we write it as 2 × 3 = 6."

1.2 Commutation

Then Pratham showed Dad a neat trick, "2 × 3 is the same as 3 × 2. We can **swap** the numbers and still get the same answer. This is called **commutation** because the numbers can travel back and forth like a commuter."

"Why does this work? Well, put 6 dots in 2 rows of three. In terms of multiplication, that's two times three. Now look at the columns, and you will see 3 columns of two, which is three times two." Mom added.

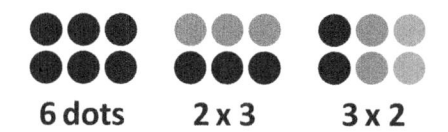

| 6 dots | 2 x 3 | 3 x 2 |

1.3 Association

"When we add numbers we get their sum; when we times, we get their product. The sum 2 + 3 + 4 is the same as 2 + (3 + 4). The product 2 × 3 × 4 is the same as 2 × (3 × 4). You can do the any group of multiplications first, but the answer will be the same. This is called association or grouping. Both addition and multiplication are associative." Pratham said.

1.4 A Multiplication Table

"But to multiply small numbers, I don't really need to add. I know a table, so I can multiply fast. I memorized its ten columns and rows. Multiples of the first ten numbers they show. The first row has multiples of one; the second row, multiples of two ... ok, let me show you. I fill each row by keep adding the first number. Then it can be memorized in any manner," Thulo began to draw:

1	2	3	4	5	6	7	8	9	10
2	4	6	8	10	12	14	16	18	20
3	6	9	12	15	18	21	24	27	30

When he was done, he also highlighted the numbers in the diagonal:

1	2	3	4	5	6	7	8	9	10
2	4	6	8	10	12	14	16	18	20
3	6	9	12	15	18	21	24	27	30
4	8	12	16	20	24	28	32	36	40
5	10	15	20	25	30	35	40	45	50
6	12	18	24	30	36	42	48	54	60
7	14	21	28	35	42	49	56	63	70
8	16	24	32	40	48	56	64	72	80
9	18	27	36	45	54	63	72	81	90
10	20	30	40	50	60	70	80	90	100

"The table will be symmetrical about the diagonal," said Pratham.

"That means the rows are the same as the columns," said Thulo.

"Let's say three times four is what I need. I just say the fourth number in the third row or column, as I please. Both numbers are twelve, as you can see, and this is the answer that I need," said Pratham.

1.5 Tables from 1 to 5

"If you remember rows one to five, you will know the tables up to five," Pratham said as he shared hints to help memorize the rows.

1s Table

| 1 | 2 | 3 | 4 | 5 | 6 | 7 | 8 | 9 | 10 |

Hint: A number times 1, is the number, itself.

2s Table

| 2 | 4 | 6 | 8 | 10 | 12 | 14 | 16 | 18 | 20 |

Hint: A number times 2, is twice the number.

3s Table

| 3 | 6 | 9 | 12 | 15 | 18 | 21 | 24 | 27 | 30 |

Hint: A number times 3 has the sum of digits 3, 6 or 9.

4s Table

| 4 | 8 | 12 | 16 | 20 | 24 | 28 | 32 | 36 | 40 |

Hint: 4s table is twice the 2s table. For example: $4 \times 3 = 2 \times 6$.

5s Table

| 5 | 10 | 15 | 20 | 25 | 30 | 35 | 40 | 45 | 50 |

Hint: 5 times an odd number ends in 5. Five times an even number is half the number followed by zero.

"Very good kids, but it's now time for bed. You can continue tomorrow," Mom said.

In a remote Himalayan temple, the Seer opened his eyes as he shut off the family scene in his mind. "Bop away little Thulo. Have fun for a while. You will need a very different type of bop, pretty soon, to survive. Both you and your brother will need this **bop**: **b**ravery, **o**ptimism, and **p**atience," he thought. "As these qualities within you grow, no problems can give you sorrow."

Practice Problems

1. Krishna, Buddha, and Jesus loved creatures great and small. If each had two pets, how many did they have in all?
2. Portland to Seattle is a three-hour drive. If Vancouver is twice as far as Seattle, how long is its drive?
3. If a dog had two fleas on each knee, how many fleas would that be?
4. If a toy costs four dollars, how many can we buy with twenty-four dollars?

Answers

1. There are $3 \times 2 = 6$ pets.
2. It will take $3 \times 2 = 6$ hours.
3. There are $4 \times 2 = 8$ fleas.
4. We can buy six, since $4 \times 6 = 24$.

Chapter 2 Horror on Halloween!

Learning to multiply up to ten

Topics *2.1 The 5 x 10 table, 2.2 Distribution, 2.3 10s times trick, 2.4 Using partners, 2.5 Tables from 6 to 10*

Early Christmas morning, as Dad sipped tea he tried to remember what had happened on Halloween. He had been handing out candy to the kids. Then one had come, dressed like a witch. She asked for thirteen dozen candies, it's true. But that is insane, wouldn't you think too?

"So many?" Dad had exclaimed. "That's 156 candies; can't you take less?"

"Huh? How did you do that so fast?" the kid had asked. "I need that many so a year it will last."

Dad hadn't replied. He had been observing the kid's toothless smile. Without even knowing, he had said out aloud "If you eat so much candy all your teeth will fall out!"

The kid got mad and in a rage she had cursed, "My teeth won't fall! You have no candy to share! It's about your math you should care! Forget all math you knew and learnt. Forget it all before the day is done!" Saying this, the kid had disappeared.

Immediately Dad had tried 97×96 in his mind. He got the answer, 9312, before a second had passed.

Then the real horror came. The morning after Halloween, there was no math in his brain. Learning of this the family became sad. But cheered up quickly when Mom said the boys could teach Dad. School was now out for the winter and the kids could sleep longer. It was only eight in the morning, but they were wide-awake. They had to teach math this winter break.

2.1 The 5 x 10 multiplication table

After breakfast, Pratham said, "To learn the tables up to five, first see how the tables divide. The right half (in bold) is the 5th column plus the left half. So just remember the left half."

1	2	3	4	5	**6**	**7**	**8**	**9**	**10**
2	4	6	8	10	**12**	**14**	**16**	**18**	**20**
3	6	9	12	15	**18**	**21**	**24**	**27**	**30**
4	8	12	16	20	**24**	**28**	**32**	**36**	**40**
5	10	15	20	25	**30**	**35**	**40**	**45**	**50**

2.2 Distribution

Thulo said, "That's actually distribution! Say I forgot the answer for three times eight. I can add $3 \times 3 + 3 \times 5$ instead. All I needed to remember was the left half to get an answer on the right half."

2.3 10s times trick

"Do you see the pattern in the last column? To multiply a number with ten, just put a zero at the end. With tricks like this we can multiply in a jiff," added Pratham.

Then Mom asked, "Pratham, if you have 7 dogs and each one had a flea, how many legs would we see?"

Pratham quickly replied, "Each dog has 4 feet, and each flea has 6. So there are 7 × 4 + 7 × 6. We can combine them as 7 × (4 + 6) to get 7 × 10 which is easier to do. So 70 is my answer for you!"

Mom reminded that we times before sum, unless the sum is in parentheses. Thus, 6 + 4 × 7 = 6 + 28 = 34; whereas (6 + 4) × 7 = 10 × 7 = 70. She also said to multiply a number by 100, just put two zeroes at the end; to multiply by a 1000, put three zeroes at the end, and so on.

2.4 Using partners

"Are there other easy ways to multiply?" asked Dad.

"We can use partners to multiply numbers between five and ten. Two numbers are partners if they add up to be ten. So, five is its own partner," Pratham said.

"How do we use this method?" asked Dad.

"Subtract the bigger number's partner from the smaller number. Then multiply their partners. To do 7 × 8 using partners, first see 8's partner is two, and 7's partner is three," Pratham said.

Then he asked Dad to do the following steps:

1. Subtract 8's partner from 7: 7 − 2 = 5.
2. Multiply the two partners: 2 × 3 = 6.
3. Put the two together, the answer is 56.

Using distribution, we could also have done:

7 × 8 = 7 × (10 − 2) = 7 × 10 − 7 × 2 = 70 − 14 = 56.

There are many ways to solve in math – pick the one that makes you fast.

Note: if the product of the partners is more than 10, we carry over. So to do 6 × 7, we get 6 – 3 = 3 and 3 × 4 = 12. Putting them together, we get 42 since we carry over the 1 from 12.

2.5 Tables from 6 to 10

Mom said, "Once you learn the 10 x 10 table, multiplication gets very simple."

"If you remember rows six to ten, you will know the tables from six to ten," Pratham told Dad as he shared hints to help memorize the rows.

6s Table

| 6 | 12 | 18 | 24 | 30 | 36 | 42 | 48 | 54 | 60 |

Hint: An even number times 6, is half the number, followed by the number itself. 6 × 2 = 12, 6 × 4 = 24, 6 × 6 = 36, 6 × 8 = 48.

7s Table

| 7 | 14 | 21 | 28 | 35 | 42 | 49 | 56 | 63 | 70 |

Hint: A multiple of 3 times 7, follows a simple pattern: 7 × 3 = 21, 7 × 6 = 42, 7 × 9 = 63. Using partners, 7 × 7 = 7-3 followed by 9 = 49; 7 × 8 = 7 – 2 followed by 6 = 56.

8s Table

| 8 | 16 | 24 | 32 | 40 | 48 | 56 | 64 | 72 | 80 |

Hint: $8 \times 6 = 6 \times 8$; $8 \times 7 = 7 \times 8$. Using partners, $8 \times 8 = 8 - 2$ followed by $4 = 64$; $8 \times 9 = 8 - 1$ followed by $2 = 72$.

9s Table

| 9 | 18 | 27 | 36 | 45 | 54 | 63 | 72 | 81 | 90 |

Hint: Using partners, $9 \times$ a number = number $- 1$ followed by the number's partner. Example: $9 \times 4 = 4 - 1$ followed by $6 = 36$; $9 \times 8 = 8 - 1$ followed by $2 = 72$.

10s Table

| 10 | 20 | 30 | 40 | 50 | 60 | 70 | 80 | 90 | 100 |

Hint: A number times 10 is the number followed by zero.

Now Mom asked Thulo, "Can you tell me how much is 14×4?"

"I can split up the multiplication using distribution," said Thulo as he did:

$14 \times 4 = (10 + 4) \times 4 = 10 \times 4 + 4 \times 4 = 40 + 16 = 56$.

"We can also do the multiplication using association," said Pratham as he did:

$14 \times 4 = (7 \times 2) \times 4 = 7 \times (2 \times 4) = 7 \times 8 = 56$.

Suddenly, Pratham became quite worried, "Mom, do you think the witch might return?"

Mom said, ruffling his hair, "No. I don't think she will dare." But silently she felt this wasn't the end. If the witch returned, how would they defend?

Practice Problem

My book has 81 pages. Each chapter has 9 pages. If I have read 3 chapters, how many chapters are left?

Answer

The book has 9 chapters since 9 × 9 = 81. So I have 9 – 3 = 6 chapters left.

Chapter 3 The Witch plans a return

Learning to add a simple series

Topics *3.1 Rearrange addition to do multiplication, 3.2 Use the 5x5 table to add a number series, 3.3 Use the 5x6 table to add a series, 3.4 General formula to add a series, 3.5 Find the Nth number of a series.*

Matya, the witch who hated math, paced up and down her cottage in her black hat. "I must go back to that house. I must go back without a doubt," she said.

"Which house, Matya?" asked Maya "What's this about?"

Her older cousin looked back, clearly displeased, "Obviously the house where I was refused treats."

"But no one gives that much candy you know. Yet every Halloween you ask for more. You should take one or two, and not curse people like you do."

"No. The man was being selfish, like all mathematicians. Serves him right to forget his Math; I hope he messes up his taxes!" Matya laughed as she imagined the man struggling with his taxes.

"That makes no sense. I am good at Math too, and I'm not selfish. Do I seem that way to you?" said Maya.

"You haven't seen the world my dear. People use math selfishly each day. They use it only for profit, I'd say. I have been hurt by the use of math. In my book, math makes people bad."

"Math doesn't make you good or bad. It's to do with one's heart, and that's the fact," said Maya.

But Matya's mind was on her scheme for revenge and she paid no attention to Maya's words. Even though they were really cousins, Maya and Matya lived like sisters. After Matya's parents had died, Maya's parents had adopted her.

3.1 Rearrange addition to do multiplication

"First help make this potion with me. I need 1+2+3+5+6+7 drops of mustard oil. Now how many drops do I need in all?" asked Matya.

"That's a simple multiplication problem. You need 24 drops of oil in all," said Maya.

"Huh? How is that multiplication? Even I know you add the same number many times when you multiply!"

Maya explained, "If I re-arrange $1 + 2 + 3 + 5 + 6 + 7$, I could turn it into multiplication: $1 + 7 + 2 + 6 + 3 + 5 = 8 + 8 + 8 = 8 \times 3 = 24$"

"By the way sis, I don't think you're looking at the recipe for a magic potion. I think this is your special chicken-in-hot-mustard-oil recipe that always upsets my stomach," Maya noticed.

3.2 Use the 5 x 5 Table to add a number series

"Okay genius, can you turn 1 + 3 + 5 + 7 + 9 drops into multiplication? I need that much of the next ingredient," Matya challenged.

"That's easy too: 1 + 3 + 5 + 7 + 9 = 5 × 5. So 25 drops is the answer for you," Maya replied.

"Huh? How is that 5 × 5? How do you know that for a fact?" Matya asked, taken aback.

"I learned it at school. The 5 x 5 table has all the clues. It can help you add a series of numbers. It really is quite clever," said Maya.

Maya drew the following tables to help explain:

The 5x5 table has 25 boxes

1	2	3	4	5
2	4	6	8	10
3	6	9	12	15
4	8	12	16	20
5	10	15	20	25

Color the table like below

This breaks the table into sections with 1, 3, 5, 7 and 9 boxes. Thus, 1+3+5+7+9 equals 25.

"As you can see, the sum of the first 'N' odd numbers is just N times N. So the sum of the first ten odd numbers is ten times ten," Maya concluded.

"Are there other series we can add?" Matya asked.

3.3 Use the 5 x 6 Table to add a series

"We can add the first 'N' numbers too. The 5 x 6 table has all the clues," said Maya.

Maya drew the following tables to help explain:

The 5x6 table has 30 boxes

1	2	3	4	5	6
2	4	6	8	10	12
3	6	9	12	15	18
4	8	12	16	20	24
5	10	15	20	25	30

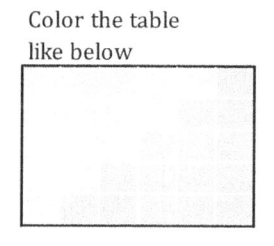

Color the table like below

This breaks the table into two halves. Each half has 1+2+3+4+5 boxes. So this sum is half of 30 and equals 15.

"As you can see, twice the sum of the first 'N' numbers is N times N plus one. So twice the sum of the first ten numbers is ten times eleven," said Maya.

3.4 General formula to sum simple series

"Is there a magic formula, one way that's easy, to find the sum of any series?" Matya asked.

"Yes there is. If the difference between a number and the next one in the series is always the same. In the series 1 + 2 + 3 + 4 + 5, this difference is one. In the series 1 + 3 + 5 + 7 + 9, this difference is two. This difference is also called the delta," Maya said.

"Hurry up then. Teach me the magic formula then!" Anything magical always interested Matya.

"I will, if you promise not to harm that family," Maya replied.

"Ok. I promise, as long as they don't provoke me. I am just creating a forgetting spell so they will never recognize me," said Matya.

"And you must take me along there," demanded Maya.

"Deal. So tell me the magic formula dear," said Matya.

"It's quite simple really. Just find the average of the first and last number in the series. The average of two numbers is half of their sum. Then multiply the average by the count of numbers in the series."

Maya showed some examples:

For the series 1 + 2 + 3 + 4 + 5,
the first number = 1.
the last number = 5.
Average of 1 and 5 is 3.
Count = 5 since there are five numbers in the series.
Sum of the series = Average × Count = 3 × 5 = 15.

For the series 1 + 3 + 5 + 7 + 9,
the first number = 1.
the last number = 9.
Average of 1 and 9 is 5.
Count = 5 since there are five numbers in the series.
Sum of the series = Average × Count = 5 × 5 = 25.

3.5 Find the Nth number of a series

"Also note the Nth number in the series = the first number + (N-1) × delta. So the fourth number in a series from 1 with delta of 3 is 1 + (4-1) × 3 = 1 + 9 = 10," said Maya.

"How is that useful?" asked Matya.

"Let's say you're reading a book, and you get faster each day, reading two more pages than the previous day. If you read four pages on the first day, you know you will read 12 on the 5th day since 4 + (5-1) × 2 = 4 + 8 = 12. And total pages read by the 5th day = average × count = half of (4 + 12) × 5 = 8 × 5 = 40."

Matya hugged Maya. "So that way I can know how fast I can finish my book. Thanks sis, but I can hear the call for dinner. Tell mom I'll be down as soon as I get this potion done. You can start without me."

Deep in the Himalayas, in the Tiger's Nest Temple, Seer Bhrigu was working on a plan too. He stretched out his hand, muttering some mantras, and a little monarch butterfly appeared out of thin air and settled on his palm. "I am sorry little friend to bring you so far from home. But you must do a small service for me, you know."

Bhrigu passed his other hand over the butterfly. It doubled in size and a glorious rainbow pattern appeared on its body. With a last loving glance Bhrigu sent the butterfly back home and it re-appeared outside Matya's window.

In a mountain cave nearby the Temple, Teninone looked up as he heard one of his spies enter. The cave was a secret entrance to Teninone's palace.

"Lord Teninone, we are wasting our time spying on Bhrigu." reported the spy. "All he does is sit and pray in the Tiger's Nest Temple. And I saw him playing with a monarch butterfly in the courtyard. He doesn't seem worried at all. I don't see any signs of an impending war."

Teninone turned crimson "You fool! Seer Bhrigu's predictions are very serious." The Demon Lord's face grew grave. "What is this about a monarch butterfly that you tell?"

"Yes, with a rainbow-colored body. It was quite pretty."

"He has been creating magic! We must capture it and find out the Seer's plan for it. And we must obtain the mind stone from him. Then I can easily overturn his prediction." Seer Bhrigu had predicted that Teninone would lose everything in an impending war.

"So why bother about an insignificant butterfly, my Lord?"

"Any threat to my power must be crushed. Bhrigu has dared to predict I will be defeated. And he teaches and practices magic here even though I have outlawed it! We must make a fool of him, punish him, and seize or destroy any magic from him!" Teninone seethed.

Practice Problem

I made a 4-story card castle. How many cards did I need?

Answer

To make a card castle we need to balance angled cards on flat ones. We can see the number of angled cards is 2 + 4 + 6 + 8 = count × average = 4 × 5. We can see number of flat cards is 1 + 2 + 3 = 6. So I needed 4 × 5 + 6 = 26 cards or half a deck of cards.

SECTION – II

Chapter 4 The butterfly effect

Learning to multiply up to twenty

Topics 4.1 Multiplying numbers between 10 and 20, 4.2 Quick method, 4.3 11s times trick, 4.4 Quick method extended

---

Pratham asked his Mom, "Why do bad things happen to good people?"

"Are you asking why God didn't protect Dad from the curse?"

"Yes, why didn't God protect him?" Pratham asked.

"God's ways can be mysterious, you know. To make good people great She puts on a show. In a crisis, we must keep faith, and stick to truth and stay compassionate. Be brave, optimistic and patient, my dear. All will be well; have no fear. Now run along and play with your brother outside. It's nice and sunny, and lunch won't be ready for a while."

Pratham went outside to find Thulo. As he walked out the door, he spotted his brother running towards a girl in a black dress and hat.

The girl tried to stop him with a frigid stare, but Thulo kept running; he didn't care. Then Pratham understood why his brother was running so happily. There was giant rainbow-winged butterfly perched on the girl's shoulder. And Thulo loved rainbows.

"Be careful Thulo! Look where you're going!" said Pratham.

Thulo did not slow down. Distracted by the rainbow colors, he ran into Matya and they both fell down!

"I'm sorry," Thulo said as they tried to get up.

Maya, who was standing next to Matya checked to see if anyone was hurt.

"Look – what a pretty butterfly," said Thulo pointing up.

Everyone looked up at the butterfly that was now giving out rainbow lights. Then they heard a voice in the sky, "Where fearlessness, love, and wisdom combine, the rainbow powers will join with thine."

The voice continued: "To Pratham who is brave, will come powers orange and red. Selflessness from orange, and fearlessness from red." Pratham saw a red-orange band form on his arm. "Bravely stand for truth and honesty. God's blessing you will derive, that is a certainty."

"To Maya with insight which is never shallow, will come the power of yellow. Yellow for knowledge like the Sun, you will see through everyone." A yellow band formed on her arm. "Knowledge will make you calm and wise. God's blessing you too will derive."

"To Thulo, with the loving heart that we have seen, will come powers blue and green. These are the colors of Mother Earth, the symbols of patience and love. This is the greatest power to possess. It transforms a heart to love from hate. Love brings selflessness. Love brings wisdom. Love is the key to Heaven's kingdom." A blue-green band formed on his arm.

"To Matya with a mind that is set, will come powers indigo and violet. Your grit to finish your plan will put time and motion at your command. You will be able to grow old or young and freeze time to get your job done. But these powers will flee from thee if you hate humanity." Matya looked for a band on her arm. She kept searching, but she could still find none.

Was there no band since her heart had nurtured hate? But Maya said smiling with glee, "Matya, your eyes, their colors have changed! One is indigo, and one is violet!"

Almost at once, Pratham and Maya spotted a form. It came out of the bushes and seemed to be armed. The man was holding what looked like a spear.

Matya and Maya however exclaimed, "Stand back. He is a demon, and may attack."

The demon was surprised. He had not expected to see witches. Avoiding a confrontation seemed the best course.

"I mean no harm witches, but you are breaking the rules. We do not out each other," said the demon.

"But rules don't apply if you come to attack," Matya said, pointing to the spear.

The demon had sensed high magic levels from the direction of the kids, but now it was gone. Something was fishy. He had to send a message to Prefect Gravemon without fail. He would assess the situation before informing Lord Teninone further.

As the kids were getting ready to shout for help, the demon disappeared as suddenly as he had come.

"Who are you and why did you say that man was a demon? Are there demons?" Pratham asked Matya.

"Yes demons exist. They look like normal humans, but their eyes don't blink. We are witches and we know how to spot them. But I have something to admit. I had come here to cast a spell but somehow I feel my heart changed after I fell. Is there someone in your house suffering from a curse?"

Pratham said hopefully, "Yes. Our dad was cursed to forget his math. So can you return my dad's memory? He has been struggling with math for a while."

Matya shook her head and sighed, "I don't know how; if I knew I might. I also need to admit I placed the curse. I would like to apologize to your family, if you will let me."

Pratham and Thulo led Matya and Maya back to their house.

4.1 Multiplying numbers between 10 and 20

As they all walked in through the door, they found Mom and Dad studying the floor. "We need to replace the living room carpet. It's quite worn," said Mom.

Mom measured to find the room was 16 feet long and 14 feet wide. She quickly calculated the area, 16 feet × 14 feet = 224 square feet. That is how much new carpet they would need.

"How did you do that so fast?" Matya asked surprised.

Dad was startled to hear the voice—it sounded like the witch's but was much sweeter and nice.

Matya now admitted—she had been the very bad witch. "I am truly sorry for what I did. But from now on, I am a friend."

Mom invited Matya and Maya to spend the day with them and get better acquainted. They were sad the curse could not be reversed, but happy to have new friends with kind hearts. Then Mom asked Pratham to show how to do 16 ×14.

Pratham said "Add the one's digit of the second number to the first number. This gives the ten's place result. Then multiply the ones digits of the two numbers. This gives the one's place result. Combine the results using carry-over."

Pratham showed the steps for 16 × 14:

1. Add the one's digit of the second number to the first: 16 + 4 = 20.
2. Multiply the ones digits of the two numbers: 6 × 4 = 24.
3. Combine the results: 20 × 10 + 24 = 224.

Similarly, 12 × 13 = 15 × 10 + 6 = 156

4.2 Quick method

"Kids, is there a quicker way to do 16 × 14?" Mom asked.

"Yes there is!" Maya replied. "Since they are between 10 and 20, and their ones digits are partners (add up to be 10), you can use a trick. Just multiply the ones digits and add 200."

Maya showed the steps for 16 × 14:

1. The one's digits of 16 and 14 are partners since 6 + 4 =10. Multiplying them, we get 24.

2. Add 200:   200 + 24 = 224.

4.3 11s times trick

Thulo was very happy to learn the quick method. "Usually, I use the 11s times trick to multiply a number by 11. I just add the two digits of the number, and place in the middle. So 11 × 14 = 1 : (1+ 4) : 4 = 154. But it's slower to do when there is a carry-over. 11 × 19 = 1 : (1+9) : 9 = 1 : 10 : 9. Then I carry over the 1 from 10 to get 209. But with the quick method, it is so easy! It's just 200 + (1 × 9) = 209!"

4.4 Quick method extended

"Thulo, this will make you real happy. The quick method works for numbers in any decade. So it will work for numbers in the 20s or 30s or 40s and so on," said Maya.

"Show me," said Thulo.

"Me too," said Matya.

"For numbers in the 20s add 20 x 30 to the ones product; for numbers in the 30s add 30 × 40 to the ones product and so on. So 23 × 27 = 600 + 21 = 621, and 29 × 21 = 600 + 9 = 609. Similarly, 33 × 37 = 1200 + 21 = 1221, and 39 × 31 = 1200 + 9 = 1209," Maya said.

"We can use this trick to square numbers ending in 5. Squaring means multiplying a number by itself. So 25 × 25 = 600 + 25 = 625, and 35 × 35 = 1200 + 25 = 1225," said Pratham. "A shorter way to write 25 × 25 is 25^2, meaning multiply 25 two times. We also read it as 25 to the power 2. Similarly 25^3 is 25 to the power 3 and is 25 × 25 × 25."

"Actually, as long as a pair (ones or tens) of digits match or one number's digits match and the other two digits add to ten, we can use this method. The general solution is to multiply the tens digits and add the matching digit. Then multiply the ones digits and combine," said Maya as she showed:

23 × 27 = (2 × 2 + 2) : 3 × 7 = 6 : 21 = 621

32 × 72 = (3 × 7 + 2) : 2 × 2 = 23 : 04 = 2304

37 × 22 = (3 × 2 + 2) : 7 × 2 = 8 : 14 = 814

Then Pratham remembered, "We have something important to tell you. A real-life demon dropped by just now. He had a spear and could've attacked, but disappeared before we could raise an alarm."

Mom and Dad listened to these words in disbelief.

"What makes you say he was a demon?" asked Mom.

Matya replied, "We witches have learned to recognize them from their eyes. They never blink. However, I don't think we need to worry. They usually remain hidden and keep their distance from witches. Actually, some government agencies know about this but don't publicize to avoid panic. There is a Central Para-normal Intelligence Agency (PIA) which helps in demon incidents."

Mom and Dad felt relieved hearing these words. Dad tried contacting the Agency and the Regional Director, Dr. Graver, answered. "I don't see much cause for concern but we will keep an eye out for any suspicious activity over the next few days," he said.

In Dr. Graver's office, Salmon waited for the call to end. "What was that about, Gravemon?" he asked.

"It was about you. I have told you many times not to go around with that spear. It attracts too much attention. And, it is not very accurate in detecting magical activity either," said Gravemon, clearly displeased. "Fortunately for you, I am also Dr. Graver, Regional Director of the PIA. We need to check out these kids, and I have a plan."

Practice Problem

Squids have 10 arms and Octopuses have 8 arms. If I count 86 arms in a group of squids and octopuses, how many of each are there?

Answer 86 arms = (Squids × 10 arms) + (Octopuses × 8 arms). Multiples of 8 that end in 6 and are less than 86, are 16 and 56. So, there could be 2 octopuses and 7 squids, or 7 octopuses and 3 squids.

Chapter 5 Friends unite

Learning to multiply up to 100 & do simple permutations and combinations

Topics *5.1 Calculate simple combinations 5.2 Factorials and Permutations 5.3 Multiplying 2-digit numbers, 5.4 Quick methods, 5.5 Difference of squares method*

The four friends spent the whole day together and talked late into the evening. Maya and Matya had received permission from home to stay late. Now they were getting ready to leave.

"This still seems unreal. Do we really have any powers? I don't feel any different. It only seems like Matya has a real power, the power to change her age. Can you try Matya?" asked Pratham.

"Let's see," said Matya. She concentrated very hard on becoming younger but nothing happened.

Thulo felt disappointed. "Maya is about Pratham's age. I want someone my age. Please become six for me, Matya."

Matya felt a strange stirring in her heart on hearing Thulo's plea and turned six in a flash!

Everyone started talking at once about the remarkable event. Meanwhile, a little distance away, four demon field agents were conspiring to capture the kids.

5.1 Calculate simple combinations

"Salmon, what you say sounds fishy!" Darkmon laughed as Salmon listened angrily. He rued the day he was given his name. Fish jokes by other demons had become his bane. "You detected strong magical activity for a brief moment, and then it was gone? And you can't even classify the power?"

"We still need to check it out. There being witches, even young ones, complicates things a bit." said Gravemon, their leader.

"How about a quick bite before we go? I can't work on an empty stomach," said Jellymon.

"How many sandwiches did you pack?" Darkmon asked.

"I have two each for all of you. And then I have a few." Jellymon replied checking the contents of his bag.

"What's a 'few' now Jellymon? Last time the bag weighed a ton!" said Salmon with a laugh.

"Jellymon, don't over-eat. I need you to be alert, and on your feet," added Gravemon, gravely. "I received information from General Greymon that Seer Bhrigu created a powerful magic at the Tiger's Nest Temple. It may have been transferred to these kids."

"Hey, I see them now. They just walked out the door. However, I see only three. I do not see the older witch," Salmon said.

"Do I have time to eat? I have four types of bread: white, wheat, oat, and rye. And three types of fillings: jelly, cheese, and egg salad. I made only one sandwich for myself, one with each combination."

"That's still a dozen sandwiches, Uncle Jelly," a small voice said from within his bag.

"What?! How did your nephew get here Jelly? Our mission can't have a snag!" Darkmon said darkly.

"I have no idea – how did you get here Peamon? How did you get in my bag?"

"I made myself tiny and entered your bag. Now that I'm here please don't send me back." Peamon pleaded.

"Okay we may let you stay, but how did you know I have a dozen sandwiches today?" asked Jellymon.

"That's easy. I multiplied. I found all the possible combinations of sandwiches. You had 4 choices of bread, and 3 choices of fillings. So total combinations = 4 × 3 = 12. That's because each type of bread has 3 possible fillings. We add 3 four times," said Peamon.

5.2 Factorials and Permutations

"Hey Uncle Jelly, let's say you ate all the sandwiches in the order of lighter to darker breads. There are still more than a thousand different orders in which you can choose to eat the sandwiches!" Peamon said.

"You don't say! How on earth can you know?" asked Jellymon.

"It's true! I used multiplication here too! You start with the White bread sandwiches. You can eat them in 6 different orders. You have 3 ways to choose the first sandwich – egg salad, cheese, or jelly. Once you ate the first sandwich, you have 2 remaining choices for the second sandwich. After the second sandwich, you have only one choice left for the third. So total orderings (also called permutations) = 3 × 2 × 1 = 6."

Note: The number of ways to order N things is the product of all numbers from 1 to N. We call the product N-Factorial, and write it as 'N!'. So 3-factorial = 3! = 3 × 2 × 1 = 6.

Peamon showed the full list of orderings (permutations):

1. Jelly, then Cheese, then Egg salad

2. Jelly, then Egg salad, then Cheese

3. Cheese, then Jelly, then Egg salad

4. Cheese, then Egg salad, then Jelly

5. Egg salad, then Jelly, then Cheese

6. Egg salad, then Cheese, then Jelly

Peamon continued, "Similarly, there are 6 orderings each for the other 3 types of bread sandwiches. So, the total different orders for eating these sandwiches = 6 × 6 × 6 × 6 = 36 × 36 = 1296."

Note: Permutations = choice combinations where order makes a difference. If Jellymon could have eaten the 12 sandwiches in any order, he could do this in 12! ways. That's almost half a billion ways! The exact number is 479,001,600.

Let's look at another example. Say we have 5 dots in a circle. How many different triangles can we form joining the dots?

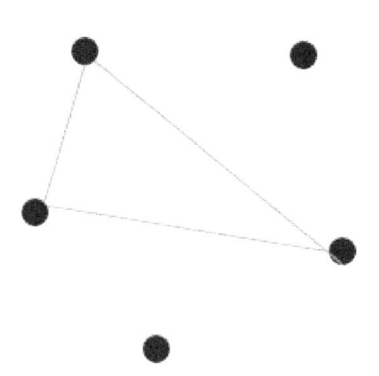

Here, you can see 3 dots, out of 5, are joined to form a triangle. To select any 3 dots, we have 5 ways to choose the first dot, 4 ways for the second dot, and 3 ways for the third dot. So we can choose 3 dots out of 5 in 5 x 4 x 3 = 60 ways.

However, no matter which order we choose a set of 3 dots (we could choose the top dot first, second or last), it is the same triangle. There are 3 x 2 x 1 = 6 orders in which we can choose the same set of 3 dots.

So total unique triangles we can make from the 5 dots = 60 / 6 = 10 triangles. This is not a permutations count; it is a combinations count.

5.3 Multiplying 2-digit numbers

Darkmon had been listening quietly. He checked the calculation on his cellphone: 36 x 36 = 1296. Peamon had calculated this faster than he could punch the numbers into his phone! "How'd you multiply so fast?" Darkmon asked, surprised.

"Well, usually we multiply the digits of the first number (called the multiplicand) with each digit of the second number (called the multiplier) shifted by its tens place. And then we add the results," said Peamon as he showed:

```
        3
    3   6                          3   6
  × 3   6                        × 3   6
  ───────                        ───────
        6                        2   1   6
```

Multiply the ones digits. Carry-over is **3**.

Cross-multiply and add the carry-over. 18 + 3 = 21.

```
    1
    3   6              3   6                  3   6
  × 3   6            × 3   6                × 3   6
  ───────            ───────                ───────
  2   1   6          2   1   6              2   1   6
        8        1   0   8              1   0   8
                                        ─────────────
                                        1   2   9   6
```

Cross-multiply Carry-over is **1**.

Multiply the tens digits & add the carry. 9 + 1 = 10

Add the rows.

"We could do this faster using the **2-line** method that goes from left to right

3 6 × 3 6 ───── 9	3 6 × 3 6 ───── 9 6 3	3 6 × 3 6 ───── 9 6 6 3 3 ───── 1 2 9 6
Multiply the tens digits and write the answer below.	Cross-multiply and sum. Write the sum, 36, diagonally.	Multiply the ones. Write the answer diagonally, and add the rows.

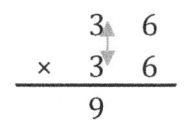

5.4 Quick methods

"But in this case I used an even faster way," Peamon explained happily. "I did 42 x 30 + 36 = 1296."

"Why don't we always use this fast method, then? And how is it done?" Darkmon asked.

"This works only when both numbers are in the same decade – like how they are in the 30s, in this case. We just need to do the following steps:

1. Add the ones digit of the second number to the first: 36 + 6 = 42.
2. Multiply this sum by the tens value: 42 x 30 = 1260.
3. Multiply the ones digits of the two numbers: 6 × 6 = 36.
4. Combine the results: 1260 + 36 = 1296.

Note: Compare how we did 16 × 14 earlier:

1. Add the one's digit of the second number to the first: 16 + 4 = 20.
2. Multiply the ones digits of the two numbers: 6 × 4 = 24.
3. Combine the results: 20 × 10 + 24 = 224.

"Are there other quick methods?" asked Jellymon.

"Yes, we could use partners. Since the numbers are in the 30s, we could use their ones-digit partners. In this case, since both numbers are 36, the partners are 4. Now we can do: 40 × (40 − sum of partners) + product of partners = 40 × (40 − 8) + 16 = 40 × 32 + 16 = 1280 + 16 = 1296. This is very useful when the ones digits are big numbers. For example, 39 × 38 is simply 40 × 37 + 2 = 1482," said Peamon.

"It is even more useful when multiplying numbers in the 90s," Peamon continued. "For example, 98 × 97 = 100 × (100 − 5) + 6 = 9506."

"Let me try. So 96 × 96 = 9200 + 16 = 9216?" asked Gravemon.

"That's right."

"Thanks for sharing this method with us Peamon. But we need to work now. We may need to capture some humans who may be a danger to us," said Gravemon.

"But, aren't they just kids? Why should you capture them?" Peamon asked.

Before Gravemon could reply, Darkmon said, "You're too young to understand. They may be possessing special powers. If humans gain powers, they will be a threat for us. We must rule over them, in secret."

Peamon looked at his Uncle in surprise. Uncle Jelly looked sad but kept quiet.

Peamon said, "But there are so many humans that are noble and fearless, so many kind and selfless, so many saints from every religion, so many scientists from every region. Why not befriend them?"

Gravemon whispered gravely to Jelly, "Keep an eye on your nephew. We don't want another Rockmon." Jellymon nodded sadly. He loved his nephew.

Twenty years before, a charismatic, impetuous and brave young demon named Rockmon had led an uprising against Teninone. He wanted demons and humans to unite. Demons did not have to be evil. Teninone was making them so. Demon really means dna-man—humans that had gained special physical powers due to mutations in their DNA.

However, the uprising was crushed. And though Rockmon was never captured; it was generally believed that he had died in battle. For no one had seen him since the uprising.

Gravemon declared, "No more talk. Now we walk. Salmon and Darkmon, accost the kids. Let's see if they display any powers."

5.5 Difference of squares method

As the two demons walked up to the house, the kids saw them. Before anyone could say a word, Darkmon released a gas from his fingers that induced fear paralysis in his victims. The kids stood motionless like statues.

"I don't see what the fuss is about," laughed Darkmon. "A simple fear paralysis and their powers, if any, are useless."

Before he could make another comment, Pratham jumped up and gave a flying kick right into the pit of Darkmon's stomach.

Darkmon fell back twenty feet through the air, and had the wind completely knocked out of him.

Salmon made a move to attack Pratham. Thulo, out of love for his brother, broke free of his paralyzing fear. He jumped higher than he had ever done before and bopped Salmon hard on the head. Salmon fell down, unconscious. Slowly, Maya also overcame the effects of the paralysis.

Gravemon and Jellymon hurried to meet the kids. Gravemon said, "Are you ok? We are from the PIA and observed the demons attacking you. I am Director Graver and this is Agent Smiles. I spoke with your parents earlier, and can give you protective custody for some time. Please call your parents." Then turning to his partner, he said, "Cuff the demons. We'll take them for interrogation."

Maya saw the two new men blinked their eyes. But something did not feel right. "Where are your other men?" she asked. Two regular humans could never overpower two demons.

"They are in hiding," said Gravemon. Immediately Maya sensed he was lying and gave a quick look to Matya whom everyone had been ignoring.

Peamon came up from behind and said, "Don't trust them. They are not here to help you. I heard their conversation. Only Seer Bhrigu, at Tiger's Nest Temple in Bhutan, can help you."

Jellymon looked up horrified as he heard these words from his nephew. "Peamon, stay out of this. If you behave so rashly I can't shield you from Teninone."

Gravemon said, "Things are not as they always seem; that boy knows nothing and is talking nonsense. Call your parents and come with us if you want to be safe."

Matya made a quick decision. She wished very hard that the four men become frozen in time, and they immediately became motionless like statues. She could sense they would remain so for an hour.

"So what were you saying?" Maya asked Peamon, as Pratham and Thulo's parents came outside to see what was happening.

Peamon was shocked to see his uncle frozen. Then he said slowly, "Will you unfreeze my uncle if I tell you everything I know?" Matya nodded.

Peamon then said, "They had planned to take you to Demon King Teninone and somehow take away your powers. But these powers are a gift from Seer Bhrigu, and he can help you further."

"What do we do when the Demons unfreeze? Is it safe to let them free?" asked Matya.

Peamon said, "Now that we're friends, leave this to me. I will help you escape cleverly. While I lead them on a wild goose chase, you should try to reach Bhrigu's place."

Dad and Mom decided that it was best for them all to go to Matya's and Maya's home. They would be safe among the witches long enough for them to arrange for visas to Bhutan where Seer Bhrigu lived.

On the way to the witches' home, Thulo asked, "So 17 x 13 is easy – 200 + 21 = 221. Is there a method for 17 x 23 or 27 x 13?"

Pratham smiled, "Hey, that's a great question. You can use the difference of squares method. Remember, the square of a number is the number times itself. Now, 17 and 23 are both 3 away from 20. Then 17 x 23 is the difference of 20 squared and 3 squared = 20 x 20 – 3 x 3 = 400 – 9 = 391."

It was quite late by the time everyone reached the place but discussions on the day's events and plans for the future went on into the wee hours of the morning.

About an hour after they had left, as the demons unfroze and got their bearings, they asked Peamon what had happened.

"I told them to see Bhrigu. But they decided to take this to the President instead. I think they are catching a flight to Washington, and you're too late to stop them," said Peamon.

"Peamon, what type of talk is this? You can't defy Teninone!" exclaimed Jellymon, even more horrified for his nephew.

"He's right. We have people in Washington and I will need to inform them of our failure. This will not bode well for any of us. This rash behavior of yours will lead nowhere. Twenty years ago, a very powerful demon, Rockmon, was killed by Teninone due to his rash actions on behalf of humans. And though you are a kid, you will be dealt with very firmly too." Salmon and Darkmon nodded their heads in agreement.

Late that night, at their home, Jellymon woke up his nephew. "Peamon, you need to join those kids and reach Bhrigu. He can save you from Teninone's wrath. I know you lied about their whereabouts, and that you know where they really are. I would guess they have gone to the witches' village since that is out of bounds for us. Now leave very quietly."

Peamon slipped out into the night to join his friends.

"Did he leave yet?" asked Gravemon on the phone.

"Yes, Peamon has just left to join his friends," answered Jellymon.

"He almost jeopardized the mission. Now it is back on track," said Gravemon with satisfaction.

Practice Problem

A small mini-van can take 6 passengers to PDX airport. If only 4 passengers boarded, how many ways could they sit?

Answer

There are 6 seats in the mini-van. Since there are more seats than passengers, we need to choose seats. The first passenger can choose a seat in one of six ways; the second, one of five; the third, one of four; and the fourth, one of three. So total ways = 6 x 5 x 4 x 3 = 18 x 20 = 360 ways.

Chapter 6 Flight to destiny

General multiplication, multiples, factors and divisibility

Topics 6.1 General multiplication 6.2 The 2-line method 6.3 Introducing negative numbers, 6.4 Modified 2-line method, 6.5 Multiples, factors and divisibility

---

6.1 General multiplication

Demons focus on harnessing the hidden powers of their bodies. Witches focus on harnessing the powers of nature. In a sense, both are scientists, but witches love nature and are very connected to it. Before heading home, Maya had surmised that Peamon might need to escape and find a way to reach them. She asked Matya to enchant the way back home so if Peamon returned, he could see his way to their home in the witches' village.

Peamon had returned to Pratham and Thulo's home and when he touched the door, he saw a note appear addressed to him. It said, if you are Peamon, please read the mantra, "Dhiyo yoh nah pracho dayat." As soon as he did, Peamon could see a map in the air. It moved with him. He smiled when he noticed the map also had information on how long it would take to reach his destination if he walked, went by bike, or went by car. This was just like Google maps. But, the estimates were wrong. Peamon could run faster than a car. He reached his destination in less than an hour, and was surprised to find everyone still awake. It was a joyful reunion when he knocked and walked in through the door.

After much discussion, the group decided that Mom and Dad would take the kids and Peamon on a flight to Bhutan. There they would meet with Seer Bhrigu and figure out what to do next. Maya's parents had contacts in the government and they would be able to get visas for the group in two days.

Two days later, the group boarded a flight to Bhutan.

"Did you know Bhutan is in the Himalayas and has an area of 14,696 square miles? Its population density is 54 people per square mile," Pratham informed them on the way.

"So 793,584 people live there? Oregon has about 4 million people, but then we also have seven times more area," observed Maya.

"How did you quickly multiply big numbers like that?" Dad asked.

"I use the 2-line method. I have had enough practice that I can do it mentally. I multiply a group of digits to find partial sums, going left to right. I add the partial sums diagonally to get the answer. You can multiply any two numbers this way," said Maya.

6.2 The 2-line method

Maya showed how she used the 2-line method:

1 4 6 9 6	Going from left to right on the multiplicand:
× 5 4	1. Multiply it with tens digit of multiplier
5 4 6 9 6 4	2. Multiply the previous digit with ones digit of multiplier
2 4 6 6 2	3. Add the two products and write diagonally, as shown
7 9 3 5 8 4	Sum the 2 lines to get the answer

Diagonal items calculated as: 5 × 1, 5 × 4 + 4 × 1, 5 × 6 + 4 × 4, 5 × 9 + 4 × 6, 5 × 6 + 4 × 9, 4 × 6.

6.3 Introducing negative numbers

"But, I actually cheated a bit. I made the multiplication simpler using negative numbers," said Maya.

"What's that? What are negative numbers?" asked Dad.

"A negative number is below zero," said Maya. "We write them with a minus sign, and to the left of zero on a number line. It tells us we are below a level. Like -10 Celsius on a snowy day in winter is 10 degrees below zero. When we add negative numbers we go further below, and when we subtract, we come back up." Then Maya showed this on a number line so it would be easier to see.

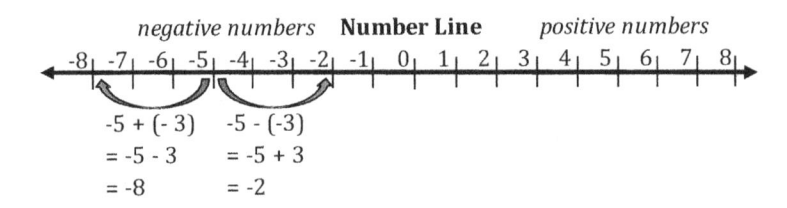

negative numbers **Number Line** *positive numbers*

-8 -7 -6 -5 -4 -3 -2 -1 0 1 2 3 4 5 6 7 8

-5 + (- 3)   -5 - (-3)
= -5 - 3   = -5 + 3
= -8   = -2

Note: that every positive number has an invisible plus sign in front. So, 2 = +2.

"An easy way to remember this is signs that are alike become plus when put together. So 5 - -3 = 5 + 3 = 8. Unlike signs when put together, become minus. So 5 - +3 = 5 + -3 = 5 – 3 = 2," said Maya.

6.4 Modified 2-line method

"Ok, so how does multiplication become simpler using negative numbers?" asked Dad.

"Well 54 is 60 − 6. So 54 can be written as 6 -6 or more clearly as 6$\bar{6}$. Using this form, multiplication becomes easier," Maya said. Then she showed:

```
    1   4   6   9   6
              ×   6   6̄
  ─────────────────────
    6 / 8 / 2 / 8 /-8 /-6
    1 / 1 / 1 /-1 /-3
  ─────────────────────
    7   9   3   7  -11  -6
```

Going from left to right on the multiplicand:
Subtract the digit on the left and multiply by 6
This is possible since the multiplier's ten digit is 6, and its ones digit is -6.
Sum the 2 lines

Diagonal items calculated as: 6 × 1, 6 × (4 - 1), 6 × (6 - 4), 6 × (9 - 6), 6 × (6 - 9), -6 × 6 . Convert to a positive number for final answer: 793700 - 116 = 793584.

6.5 Multiples, factors and divisibility

As the group boarded the flight, Maya said, "Let's sit in row 45, so we can all sit together."

Dad asked, "How do you know that Maya?"

"I know. She listened to the announcement and then found the LCM of 5 and 9, Dad," said Pratham.

"LCM? And what announcement?" Dad asked.

"LCM means Least Common Multiple. It is the smallest number that is a multiple of all the given numbers. And there was an announcement being made when you went to the restroom. We have an empty flight. Every 5th row has the three left side seats empty, and every 9th row has the middle four seats empty. Forty-five is the LCM of 5 and 9. So the 45th row is the first row that will have the left and middle seats empty – seven seats in all, just what we need." Pratham explained.

"So how does one find the LCM?" Dad asked.

"Let me answer," said Maya. "When you multiply a group of numbers together you get a multiple of all those numbers. But it will be the smallest multiple possible only if the numbers do not have any common factors. So the LCM of 4, 6, and 8 is not 4 × 6 × 8 = 192. Instead, it is 24."

"To find the LCM, we need to break up the numbers into their prime factors. These are numbers like 2, 3, 5, 7, 11, 13, etc. Numbers that can't be created as a product of any other two numbers except one and themselves. So, to find the LCM, we first write the numbers as products of their prime factors.

4 = 2 × 2

6 = 2 × 3

8 = 2 × 2 × 2

Then take the largest sequences of prime factors and multiply them together. In this case, there are only two types of prime factors – 2 and 3. The largest sequence of 2s is 2 × 2 × 2. The largest sequence of 3s is just 3. So the LCM = 2 × 2 × 2 × 3 = 8 × 3 = 24."

Thulo had been listening intently to the conversation. As they sat down in their seats, he said, "I get it now! I have swimming on every 2nd day of the week, and my friend has it every 3rd day. So using LCM, we will always meet on the 6th day. That's why I always see him on Saturdays!"

"Very good Thulo," Mom said. "But like LCM, there is another useful number. I use it all the time to make gift boxes for family and friends. Do you want to know about it?"

"Yes, I do," said Thulo as his eyes sparkled with interest.

"This number is the GCF – the Greatest Common Factor. Now, all my gift boxes must have the same number of items so no one gets less. This year I wanted to put pencils, erasers, and craft paper in each box. I had 24 pencils, 12 erasers, and 30 sheets of craft paper. Six is the largest number that is a factor of 24, 12, and 30. It is their GCF. So I can make 6 gift boxes, with each box having 4 pencils, 2 erasers, and 5 sheets of craft paper."

"But how can you tell that 6 is a factor of these numbers?" asked Dad.

"You use the same method as finding LCM, but find the longest sequences of prime factors that are also common to the numbers," said Mom. "Thulo, can you show Dad?"

"Sure," said Thulo as he showed:

24 = 2 × 2 × 2 × 3

6 = 2 × 3

12 = 2 × 2 × 3

All the numbers have one 2 and one 3 in their list of prime factors. So GCF = 2 × 3 = 6."

"How do you find the prime factors of a number?" asked Dad.

Peamon had been listening quietly. Now he said, "I use divisibility rules. They tell if a number is a factor of another number – that it can divide the other number. Dividing is the opposite of multiplying. Since 2 times 3 is 6, if we divide six items into 2 groups, each group will have 3 items," said Peamon.

Then Peamon listed out the divisibility rules for prime numbers:

Prime Factor	A number has this prime factor if ...	Example Number	Explanation
2	It is even (ends in 0, 2, 4, 6, or 8)	32	32 ends in 2.
3	Sum of digits is a multiple of 3	78	7 + 8 = 15, a multiple of 3.
5	It ends in 0 or 5	100	100 ends in 0.
7	Difference between 2 × one's digit and rest of the number, is a multiple of 7	154	15 - 4 × 2 = 15 - 8 = 7.
11	Sums of alternate digits are equal	1353	1 + 5 = 3 + 3.

"I can understand the rules for 2 and 5 since I see these patterns in their tables. But I can't see why the other rules work," said Dad.

"I can explain how to get the divisibility rule for 3. Take any 2-digit number. It is 10 × digit1 + digit2. For example, 54 = 10 × 5 + 4. If this number is divisible by 3, then if we subtract 9 × digit1 from it, the remainder is divisible by 3 too. This remainder is just digit1 + digit2, which is the sum of the digits. We can extend this logic to all numbers. The rules for 7 and 11 can be found similarly," said Peamon.

"Nice. That wasn't too hard to understand. Thank you Peamon," said Dad.

All buckled their seat belts as the plane got ready to take off. This flight would shape their destiny.

Practice Problems

1. A group of trolleys are waiting to take luggage to an airplane at PDX airport. 24 big suitcases and 18 small bags need to be taken by the trolleys. If each trolley carries the same number of suitcases and bags, how **light** can they be?
2. You have 20 red, 12 white, and 16 blue balloons. At most, how many identical bunches of balloons can you make?

Answers

1. There are 24 big suitcases and 18 small ones. To get the trolleys to be lightest, we need to find the maximum number of trolleys with identical bunch of suitcases. This maximum number of identical bunches is the GCF. The GCF of 24 and 18 is 6. With 6 trolleys, each one will have 4 big and 3 small suitcases, and this will be the lightest combination.
2. The largest number of identical bunches of balloons is the GCF of 20, 12 and 16, which is 4.

Chapter 7 Friend or foe

Multiplication to find area of shapes

Topics *7.1 Areas of squares, rectangles, and triangles 7.2 Areas of polygons and circles 7.3 Maximum area & minimum perimeter, 7.4 Petalgons and stretched shapes, 7.5 Areas using average lengths*

7.1 Areas of square, rectangles, and triangles

Their flight finally landed at the beautiful Paro International Airport, nestled in the Himalayas.

As the group entered the airport, a distinguished looking man with a flowing white beard and ochre robes came up to them with a greeting. "Are you coming from the United States to meet Seer Bhrigu?" he asked gently. "He is expecting you."

The group was surprised to see that they were expected. "Yes, we are here to meet him. How did you know? Can you take us to him?" asked Mom.

"Yes, yes. Seers are clairvoyants. They can see events happening far away or even in the future. The visions may not give the exact time, but Seer Bhrigu sensed you would arrive this week. Please come with me. It is a short ride to the temple, and I have a car waiting outside as you can see," Seer Shukra replied. He looked like a sage, and had he said so, they would have believed him to be Seer Bhrigu himself.

Everyone eagerly went along with the sage – they would soon meet Seer Bhrigu at Tiger's Nest Temple!

The "car" was more like a limousine and had windows in many shapes – triangles, circles, squares and rectangles. All the windows, except the rectangle, were the same width. Thulo said, "I want to sit next to the biggest window!"

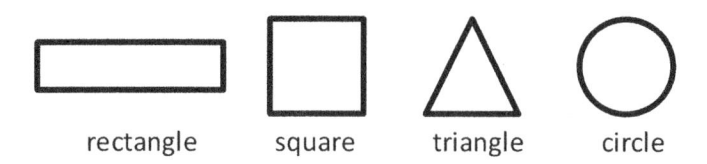

rectangle   square   triangle   circle

The circle and triangle were clearly smaller than the square as they could fit inside it. But Thulo didn't know how to compare the square and rectangle. They didn't fit in each other.

"Is the square window bigger or the rectangle one?" Thulo asked his brother.

"Remember how we calculated the area of our carpet? We did length × width. The square window is twice as tall as the rectangle one, but the rectangle one is twice as wide. So their areas are the same."

"I want to sit next to the rectangle window so I can see wider," said Thulo as he sat down next to it.

With everyone seated, the Limo started. Then Maya asked, "But do you know if the circle window is bigger than the triangle window, Thulo?"

"No. How do you find their areas?" asked Thulo.

"A triangle's area is easy to find. It is half the area of its outer rectangle. So these three triangles have the same area = half of length × height," said Maya as she drew on her phone:

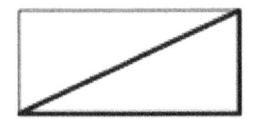

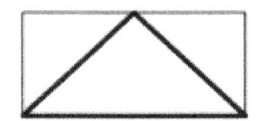

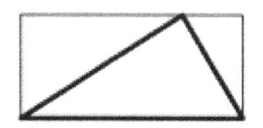

"How do you know all these triangles are half the area of the outer rectangle?" asked Thulo.

"The diagonal of a rectangle divides it in half. So, the first triangle is half the area of the outer rectangle. For the other two triangles, draw a vertical line from the top point to the base. The line divides the figures into two rectangles. The triangle's edges divide these two rectangular portions in half. So the total area of the triangle is half of the outer rectangle as well," said Maya.

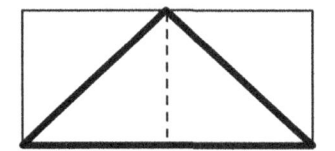

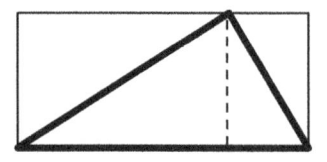

"And how about the circle's area?" asked Thulo.

7.2 Areas of polygons and circles

"Before that, do you know how important a triangle is?" asked Pratham. "We can make any polygon, any shapes with straight edges, by joining triangles together." Pratham took out his phone and drew:

square   pentagon   hexagon
= 2 △   = 3 △   = 4 △

Number of triangles needed = Number of sides of polygon -2

"And if it is a regular polygon, where all sides are equal, and you can draw an inner circle that touches each side, then the radius of this circle is called the apothem. The area of these polygons is simply half the apothem × total side length. The total side length is also called the perimeter." Pratham drew some regular polygons and their apothems (incircle radius lines).

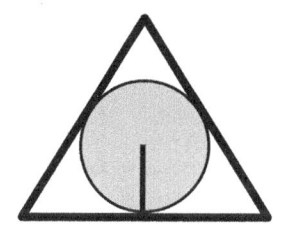

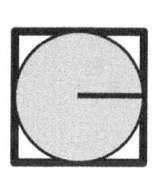

"Notice how as we increase the number of sides of the polygon, its area becomes closer to the circle inside. Since a circle is like a polygon with infinite sides, its area is then half the radius × perimeter," said Pratham.

"We also call the circle's perimeter its circumference, and it is about six times the radius. So the area is simply about 3 × radius^2," added Maya.

7.3 Maximum area, minimum perimeter

"Let's say I make a shape by joining the ends of a string. I could make a triangle, a square, a regular pentagon, or a circle. Which shape would have the most area?" Peamon asked.

"I think I can answer that," replied Maya. "All the shapes will have the same perimeter. As we increase the number of sides, the edges move away from the center of the shape. That means the apothem increases, and hence the area increases as well. Since the circle can be thought to be a polygon with infinite sides, it has the largest area," Maya answered.

"You got it!" said Peamon. The kids continued talking and laughing in this manner. As the car was nearing the temple, they did not notice the driver turn away from the main road. Seer Shukra secretly signaled the driver to take the car to Teninone's mountain cave palace.

7.4 Petalgons, and stretched shapes

Peamon noticed three blue tattoos on the driver's arm: a star-like petalgon, an ellipse, and a rhombus. He asked the driver, "What are those tattoos on your arm?"

The driver smiled back through his dark glasses, "Oh, I just like shapes so I got some tattoos of my favorite ones."

TATTOO SHAPES

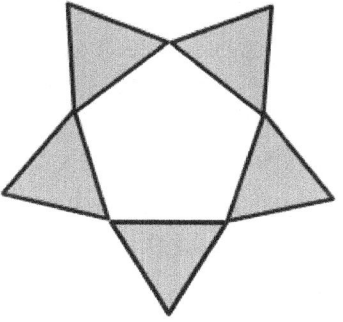

A five petal **petalgon**. If you fold the petals it will cover the pentagon inside.

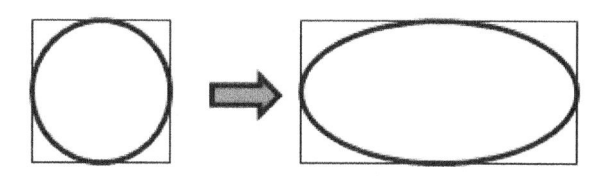

Stretch a circle to form an **ellipse**
The ellipse's area scales to the circle like their outer rectangles.
The ellipse is twice as large as the circle since its outer rectangle is twice as large as the circle's.

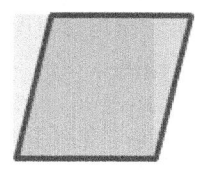

Shear a square to make a **rhombus**.
When we shear a shape, the area remains the same. It's like we cut off a triangle at the left of the square and placed it on the right.

Peamon remembered a conversation he had had with his Uncle. "Why do Salmon and Darkmon have those blue tattoos?" he had asked.

"They used to be soldiers in Teninone's army. All his soldiers have tattoos to show what powers they have. They are now spies rather than soldiers, but they still kept their tattoos," Jellymon had replied.

Peamon nudged Maya and tried to gesture to her that something was wrong. Maya found that she could peep into Peamon's mind. The experience came as a shock to her. It was as if her mind had united with Peamon's and she could feel his anxiety and read his thoughts.

"I need to go to the bathroom. Can we stop somewhere?" asked Maya.

Pratham was impatient to meet Seer Bhrigu. "Can't you wait till we reach the Temple?" he asked.

"I need to go now!" said Maya creating a big fuss and punching Pratham on the shoulder.

"Ow! You're almost as bad as Thulo," said Pratham, still oblivious of the hints Maya was trying to give him.

"Hey, I don't punch you!" protested Thulo as he punched Pratham's other shoulder.

"Good grief! That's just great," said Pratham, visibly annoyed while rubbing his shoulders. Then his eyes met Maya's and he understood she was carrying out a plan.

"Ok, maybe I could use a bio-break too," said Pratham.

Mom and Dad requested the driver to stop the car at a small store they had spotted up ahead.

Seer Shukra and the driver remained in the limo. Seer Shukra was confident of their success. He had seen a vision where he delivered the kids to Teninone.

In the store, Maya explained Peamon's concern. Matya, who had come out of the airport as a six year old, decided that this was a good time to test her powers again. She walked up to the car and as the two men seated there gazed idly at her, they turned motionless like statues.

Dad and Peamon (who could grow tall), dragged the two men from the front of the car and put them in the rearmost seats. Dad took a seat behind the wheel and Mom entered "Tiger's Nest Temple" into her cell phone's GPS program. Everyone took their seats and in a short time reached the base camp leading to the Temple.

At the camp, they saw a beautiful prayer wheel near which a number of people were standing. Asking around they found out that it would be a strenuous 7km trek up the mountain to reach the Temple. But it would also be a magical experience. At the halfway point, there was a beautiful cafeteria where one could get food, freshen up, rest, or meditate.

7.5 Finding areas using average length

As Mom and Dad were wondering if they should leave the car and begin the trek, an elderly man with a slender walking stick greeted them.

"Looks like you are on a family vacation. Do you need a tourist guide? I know all about the Taktsang Temple, also known as Tiger's Nest Temple. I can be your guide for a very reasonable fee. I will help you take pictures of the best views and make sure you have a wonderful experience."

"We thank you for your offer, but we are here to see a friend. Do you know where we can find Seer Bhrigu?" asked Mom.

"Seer Bhrigu is your friend?" the man asked. "Then you must be very unfortunate people indeed. I have not seen a single friend of his who was not in some sort of trouble. I would recommend staying away from that fellow. He is simply bad news. I haven't earned much as a guide ever since he came here a couple of months ago," the man complained.

"That's not nice to say. And we're not unfortunate, we are blessed with powers," Thulo blurted out.

"Yes, powers of observation to know who is good or bad," Maya added hastily to avoid further discussion on the topic.

The old man eyed Thulo suspiciously. "What can you do if I just bop you on the head?" The man bopped Thulo, not too hard, but with enough force to be annoying.

The group knew they should keep their powers hidden. However, before anyone else could say or do anything Thulo had already made a superhuman jump into the air, and was getting ready to come down and bop the annoying old man on the head.

However, when Thulo landed, he had somehow missed the man. Suddenly, he received another bop on the head! The man had moved so quickly, no one saw it happen. But Thulo felt it.

Maya sensed something was not right about this man. Did his eyes blink? Was he one more of Teninone's demons? She tried to read into his mind. But her mind received a hard blow, and she sat down with a splitting headache.

"It's not nice to peep," said the old man laughing.

Matya got angry seeing her sister hurt. She hated the man's laughter. He needed to be taught a lesson. She focused hard to freeze him in time. It did not work.

"Hate never helps," said the guide as he kept laughing.

Peamon moved to help his friends. Mom and Dad tried to tell him to stay back. But he had made up his mind to confront the stranger. Strangely, with each step he took, he grew smaller and smaller! And he couldn't control it.

"You should learn to listen to grown-ups sometimes," said the guide.

Pratham, who had been carefully observing, decided the man was actually dangerous. He felt the man's stick was the source of some strange power. Pratham tried to creep up to grab the man's stick.

The man saw him and said, "You're too late. What's the use of being fearless and strong if you are not quick to act?"

As the kids were in a quandary what to do next, Mom and Dad went up to the man and bowed down reverentially. "Please help us Seer Bhrigu. We have come from very far for your help."

"You got me – but keep it secret. Teninone tries to keep a watch on me at all times. I give his spies the slip with my disguise as a tourist guide. As for helping you, I have brought you here through very careful planning to help me," smiled Bhrigu.

"Help you?" asked Mom and Dad in unison.

"Yes, but more on that later. I see Seer Shukra and his driver are waking up. We will all take a trek to the Taktsang Cafeteria. Before we go, I have delicious cheeses for everyone."

Seer Bhrigu took out a box of cheeses. "These are Chhurpi, a special Himalayan cheese made from yak's, goat's, or cow's milk. Hikers take them as an ideal snack to give their bodies energy and warmth and help them climb better at these high altitudes. I also have a special green dipping sauce from herbs that is fun to take with the Chhurpi. It makes the Chhurpi ten times more effective in giving you warmth and the energy to trek."

Thulo looked with interest at the cheeses. They were shaped like pyramids, cones, cylinders, and hemi-spheres. "Could you please pass me some cheese Mom?" he asked.

"Which one do you want? The pyramid shaped one?" asked Mom.

"Which one is the smallest? I want the shape that's the smallest," said Thulo not sure if he would like it.

"Why not the one you can cover with the most sauce?" Pratham asked. He knew Thulo loved to dip cheese in ketchup.

"Which one's that?" asked Thulo.

"For that you need to know which one has the most surface area. How do you find the surface area of a pyramid, cone, cylinder, or hemi-sphere? You multiply the average perimeter by the length of the surface," said Pratham.

"I don't get it. How does that work?" asked Thulo, a little puzzled.

"Ok. Let me explain. Do you remember how we know the area of a triangle is half of length × height? There is another way to find this using a sum of series method." Pratham drew a triangle on his cell phone and explained:

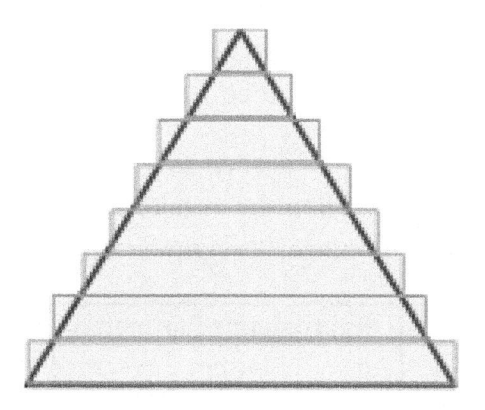

The area of the triangle ~ (is approximately equal) to the sum of the areas of the stacked rectangles. The thinner the rectangles, the closer the two areas will match, and the top rectangle's length will approximate to 0.

Total area of rectangles = Rectangle Height × (length1 + length2 + length3 ... + lengthN), where N is the number of rectangles.

Since the lengths decrease from base to top by a fixed delta, the sum of lengths = count × average length = N × half of (0 + base length).

So total area = Rectangle Height × N × half of base length = half of triangle's length × height! (just like we found before).

"For a 2D shape, a shape that is flat, like a triangle, the area is average length × height. Similarly, for 3D shapes, it is the average perimeter × the length along surface. But this is only if the difference between consecutive lengths or measures is the same. Remember the delta must be the same to use a sum of series method," said Pratham.

"We can use this method for cones. The surface area of a cone is average perimeter × length, **L**, the slant distance. At the bottom of the cone, the perimeter is ~ 6 × radius, **r**. At the top, it is zero. So the average is 3 × r. The curved surface area of the cone is then 3 × r × L," Pratham explained.

"Hey, I got an idea. If a circle is seen as a flattened cone, the slant length is just the radius. Then the area of the circle is ~ 3 × r × r = 3 × r^2, like we found before!" exclaimed Thulo.

Shape		Approximate Perimeter			Curved Area (approximate)
		Top	Bottom	Average	
Cone		0	6 × r	3 × r	3 × r × L
Cylinder		6 × r	6 × r	6 × r	6 × r × h

"But a hemisphere's curved surface area is trickier to find," said Maya. "The perimeters do not change by the same amount as you go vertically up in height. The average perimeter is not the perimeter at half the height. Instead, it is at a point half way up the curved surface. But we can still find the surface area as so," said Maya as she began to draw on her phone to show Thulo.

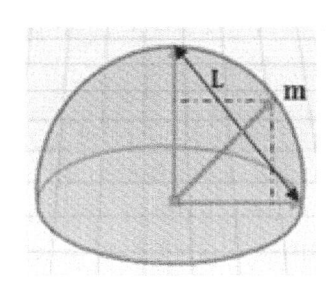

m, the mid-way point along the curve, is equidistant from the horizontal and vertical radii (in blue).

The radius, **r**, is about one and a half times this distance.

L, the slant length is about one and a half times the radius.

"So the average perimeter times the slant length, L, is about **6 × radius × radius** as the one and a half times factors cancel out. The cool thing is, the radius is also the hemisphere's height, and so the formula can become 6 × radius × height, which is the same as for a cylinder of the same height and radius!"

Seer Shukra who had been sitting sullenly now exclaimed in disgust, "Foiled by inexperienced little kids!"

Thulo looked angrily at the Seer, "We are mature. And you...you are manure!"

"Thulo, I think you meant immature," whispered his brother.

"No I meant manure. He is manure!" shouted Thulo.

Dad decided to calm Thulo down by bringing his mind back to the snacks. Most of the kids had already started eating.

"Well we don't have anything to measure the cheeses, so how do we figure out which one has the most surface area, Thulo?" asked Dad.

Thulo cheered up and exclaimed, "I know how! I will dip the cheeses in ketchup and roll them on paper napkins. Then I can compare the areas." Mom always carried ketchup pouches for Thulo.

Pratham smiled, "Thulo always finds a way to play with colors; even if it's only ketchup!"

Thulo dipped the cone and cylinder shaped cheeses in ketchup and rolled them out on paper napkins. The cylinder made a shape that looked bigger. The hemisphere shaped cheese had the same radius as the cylindrical one. Since the cylinder was taller, it had more surface area.

"The cylinder shaped cheese is the one with the most surface area," concluded Thulo as everyone clapped.

Practice Problems

Nations rise when exceptional leaders come; leaders who love their people and have strong values. One such leader was the great Franklin D. Roosevelt who served a record 4 terms as US President from 1933 to 1945. He introduced laws to help the poor, the unemployed and elderly. He brought development and added controls to stop misuse of money. We see the same values and strengths today in the Indian Prime Minister, Shri Narendra Modi.

Both have had glasses. If Roosevelt's prince-nez glasses were circles with diameter 4 cm, and Modi's glasses are trapeziums 3 cm tall and 5 cm wide at the middle, whose glasses are bigger?

Note: the diameter of a circle is it width, and equals twice the radius.

Answer

Roosevelt's glasses have a lens size $\sim 3 \times \text{radius}^2 = 3 \times 2^2 = 12$ square cm.

Modi's glasses have a lens size= height × average width. = 3 × 5 = 15 square cm, since the average width of a trapezium is its width at the middle (do you see why?).

So Modi's glasses are bigger.

Chapter 8 The mind stone's owner

Multiplication to find volumes of shapes

Topics *8.1 Volumes of prisms and cylinders, 8.2 Summing squares series, 8.3 Volumes of pyramids and cones, 8.4 Volumes of spheres and hemispheres*

8.1 Volumes of prisms and cylinders

The kids ate their fill of the cheeses and felt quite energized. They could climb any mountain now. Dad tried to get a handful, but Mom reminded him that he was watching his weight. Dad took two pieces instead.

"Kids, now that you are here, I will be able to make your powers permanent. The Taktsang Café is an hour's trek up the mountain. Once we reach there, you will see beautiful seats for meditation. Sitting on those seats, once you repeat a special mantra, your powers will become permanent," said Seer Bhrigu.

"So I guess there is no longer any point in my taking the kids to Teninone. He will not be able to take away their powers," said Seer Shukra. But in his mind, Shukra was puzzled about the vision he'd had of taking the kids to Teninone.

Seer Bhrigu nodded. Then he said, "Alright, let's all head up to the Taktsang Café. There is another more important reason to go there. The time has come for me to hand over the mind stone to its new owner," said Seer Bhrigu.

"The mind stone?!" exclaimed Seer Shukra. "You consider one of these kids more worthy than me?" Seer Shukra's face was red with anger. This reminded him of the day the Demi-Gods had insulted him. Even though he was clearly more brilliant, they chose Brihaspati to be their Advisor-in-Chief. In revenge, Shukra had gone over and accepted the position of Advisor-in-Chief for the Demons. He had made them more powerful than the Demi-Gods, and Teninone was now at the height of his power.

"It is not that. You would have been way more worthy had it not been that your allegiance lies with Teninone," said Seer Bhrigu with kindness. "My conscience does not allow me to give it to you. However, the new owner may decide to hand it over."

Seer Shukra's eyes sparkled as he now saw a possibility of getting Teninone the mind stone. "Will you allow me to take the kids to Teninone? If the new owner finds him worthy, which I am sure he will, the demons will leave them alone."

Seer Bhrigu said, "As long as you assure their safe return to me, I will allow it."

"You have my word. Take the kids to the Café. I will wait for your return here."

Seer Bhrigu turned to Mom and Dad and said, "There is nothing to worry about. Seer Shukra will not let any harm come to the kids."

The group reached the Café after an hour on the trail. Seer Bhrigu arranged for suja for everyone. He said it was a buttery tea drink. Mom was very happy to get tea. She took a sip eagerly.

"Is this tea? Why is it salty?" she asked. Nevertheless, she kept sipping—it was like a savory soup.

"This is a special Himalayan tea made with yak butter and salt. It is a healthy drink," said Bhrigu.

Pratham liked adventure, but not in his beverages. "It looks good, but I'm not that thirsty," he said.

"You should try new things," said Dad.

Peamon took a sip. "Hey, this is quite good!" he said. "You really should try it."

"Ok. I will take the smallest cup," said Pratham. He looked at the cups. Some were short cylinders and others were square prisms. The diameter of the circular cup equaled the diagonal of the square cup. Though the latter was taller, Pratham chose it.

"Why did you pick the square cup? How is it smaller?" asked Matya.

"It has less volume," said Pratham.

"What's volume?" asked Thulo.

"It's the space an object can hold or occupy. Look at this cup. Its base is a square. If we stack such squares one on top of another to the height of the cup, the stack would have the same volume. So the volume of this cup is the area of its base times its height," said Pratham.

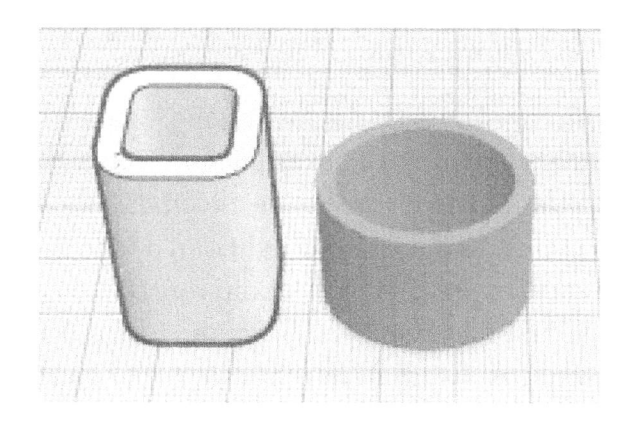

"The volume for the other cup is also the area of its base times its height. The area of a circle is about one and a half times the area of the square inside. So the circular base is about one and half times larger than the square base. The square cup is less than one and half times the height of the circular cup. This means, overall, the cup with the square base has less volume," Pratham added.

"What if the mouths of the cups were bigger than their bases—then how would we find their volumes?" asked Matya who now had a renewed interest in math.

"To know that, you first need to know how to sum the squares of a series of numbers," said Maya.

8.2 Summing squares series

Maya began to teach Thulo and Matya, "We know how to sum an arithmetic series. In a similar way, we can sum a series of squares. The formula is 3 × sum of squares = sum of numbers × 2 × (count + 1). Let me explain by adding the squares of the first four numbers. Now, according to this formula, $3 \times (1^2 + 2^2 + 3^2 + 4^2) = (1 + 2 + 3 + 4) \times (2 \times 4 + 1) = 10 \times 9 = 10 \times 3 \times 3$. So, $1^2 + 2^2 + 3^2 + 4^2$ is simply $10 \times 3 = 30$."

"Why does this formula work?" Matya asked.

"I can explain by drawing on my phone," said Maya. "I am drawing a rectangle that is 10 boxes tall and 9 boxes wide. Now I have colored the boxes to break the rectangle into 3 sections: two green sections on the left and right and a blue section in the middle. As you can see, each section represents the sum of squares of the first four numbers. From the figure, it is clear that **3 × sum of squares = sum of numbers × (2 × count + 1)**."

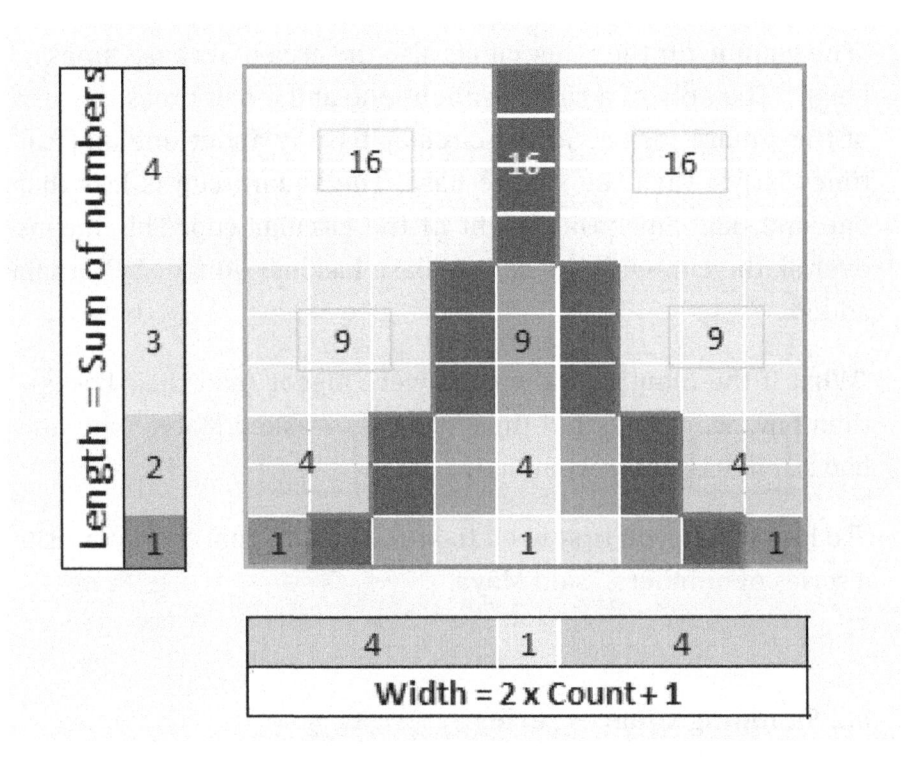

"If we stack squares of decreasing widths but same thickness, the volume of the resulting pyramid will be sum of the volumes of each square slice. These volumes form a squares series since they change as width^2. If we stack circles similarly, their volumes would also form a squares series since they change as radius^2."

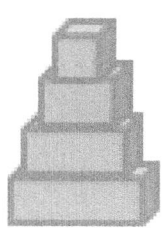

8.3 Volumes of pyramids and cones

"But, here is the cool thing. If we make each slice very thin so we get smooth edges, the stacks form pyramids and cones (see below). In this case, the count becomes very large, and the formula, gets simplified to **3 × sum of volumes = sum of widths × 2 × count × slice height = width² × height of pyramid**," said Maya.

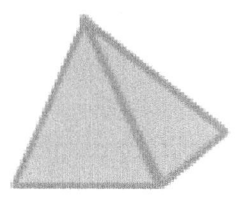

$$3 \times \text{Volume of pyramid (or cone)} = \text{base area} \times \text{height}$$

$$\text{So, Volume of cone} \sim \text{radius}^2 \times \text{height}$$

"Base area × height is the volume of a rectangular prism. That means, we can cut any such prism into 3 identical pyramid shapes!" Matya observed.

"Yes, and now I can show you how to calculate the volumes of cups that have more of a pyramid-like or conical shape. Since they can be formed by subtracting a smaller pyramid (or cone) from a larger one, their volumes are simply the difference of these two volumes," said Maya and showed:

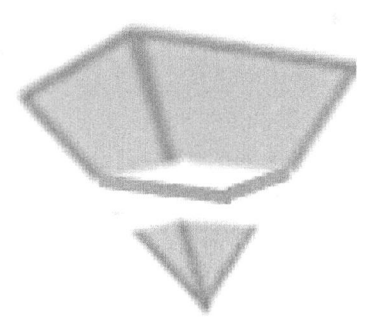

Invert the pyramid or cone and slice off the bottom to create the cup. Volume of the cup is simply the volume of the original pyramid minus the volume of the smaller cut-off pyramid," said Maya.

Seer Bhrigu now motioned for everyone to follow him. He led the kids to a secluded spot with meditation seats. He asked Pratham, Thulo, Maya, and Matya to each choose a seat and sit cross-legged and upright. Then one-by-one he whispered a mantra into their ears and they each fell into a deep state of meditation.

Turning to Peamon, Bhrigu said, "Your sense of justice is remarkable. You went against your own people to help these kids. Great demons of the past like Vibhishan and Prahlad also had this nature and were intensely devoted to God. No weapon could injure them. God protected them at all times. Wear the amulet I am giving you. As long as you wear it, no weapon can injure you either."

Peamon was very happy to get the amulet and he wanted to show it to the others – but they were still meditating. Ten minutes went by and Peamon began to feel bored. "How long will this take?" he asked "Don't we need to face Teninone too?"

"All in good time. However, you are not going. You will stay here," said Bhrigu.

"Why? I am not leaving my friends," protested Peamon.

"Your uncle wants to keep you safe. Teninone must not know who you are. It is better you stay away from him now."

"Are you talking about my Uncle Jelly? How do you know him?" Peamon asked. Peamon was surprised the Seer knew his uncle. "Anyway, he worries too much and gets afraid easily – "

"Gets afraid easily?" interrupted Bhrigu. "Why he is the bravest demon I know today."

Peamon stared blankly. Was the Seer really talking about his Uncle Jelly?

"But it's too early for that story now. You will know all in good time."

"Enough of this, 'all in good time business,'" Peamon groaned mentally.

Just then, the other kids started regaining normal consciousness.

"Your powers are strengthened and permanent," said Seer Bhrigu. "Maya, I feel that you are ready now. There is a magical stone known as the mind stone. With it, you can hypnotize a large group of people. They will see and hear any illusion you create in their minds. They will also do your bidding as long as they have the tiniest inclination to obey the command. I have been its owner for so long. Now I wish to hand it to you."

Mom said, "That is a big responsibility. Can you handle it Maya? Seer, should you not give the stone to someone older, like Matya?"

"They are all noble kids and will not misuse the power. However, Maya can see into other's minds. And that will give her an edge in efficiently using the mind stone," said Bhrigu.

Just before it started getting dark, Bhrigu led everyone back to Seer Shukra. As promised, the four kids boarded the limousine and went off to meet Teninone. Seer Shukra said he would return them before dinner.

8.4 Volumes of spheres and hemispheres

It was a short ride to Teninone's mountain cave. The cave entrance was camouflaged so no one could see it from the road. It was a big entrance, and the limo easily drove through it. Once inside, the limo stopped, the kids got out and followed Seer Shukra through secret tunnels to a large room with many soldiers standing in formation.

A man in a regal dress and with an air of command walked up to them. He had a friendly smile and asked the kids if they wanted anything to eat. The kids politely declined.

The man began to talk about himself. "You see these soldiers? Like this, I have thousands of people who work for me -- soldiers, lawyers, politicians, scientists, accountants, etc. I run many organizations with complete discipline so work gets done exactly as it should and when it should. These organizations do a tremendous amount of good." The man kept boasting in this vein for some time.

Then he said, "I learn from Seer Shukra that one of you has the mind stone. As you can clearly see, it would be of much greater benefit if I were the owner of the stone. There is so much more I could do for the world."

"Why do you have this dingy secret lair? And why have you been trying to steal the stone for so many years? Why do I feel that you are an egotistic smooth talker? I think you are the type of person who will readily misuse its power," said Pratham.

"You are too young to understand these things. You are but a child and thinking nonsense. I have power, intelligence, and experience. I deserve to be the owner of the mind stone," said the man.

Maya guessed the man was Teninone. "Why should you be the owner? Why not Seer Shukra?" asked Maya.

"That's a very good question. As you may know the mind stone can make people do your bidding —but first the people need to be receptive to your command. I rule thousands of people who are waiting to follow any order I give them. It will be very easy for me to control their minds," said Teninone.

"That makes sense, but if they are already willing to follow your orders, why do you need the stone?" Maya asked.

"Sometimes fear or other emotions prevent them from following through on my orders. In those cases the stone would help," said Teninone.

Maya could see Teninone was actually afraid that people might not follow some of his cruel orders due to their conscience. He wanted to use the mind stone's power to rule the world. He would make his armies ruthlessly crush any nation that refused to accept his supremacy.

"I think you should forget about the stone, we are not going to give it to you," said Pratham determinedly.

"Enough delay! Hand me the mind stone, kids, and you won't get hurt," Teninone said. The Demon King had been desperately seeking the mind stone for years. With it, he could bend minds to his will.

The four kids stood quietly in Teninone's Royal Hall; unafraid, though surrounded by demon soldiers.

Teninone surveyed the kids' faces to see which one would be most likely to talk. It could be the little girl, Matya, with the funny eyes; or maybe the older girl, Maya, who seemed persuadable. Could it be the older boy, Pratham, their spokesperson? But it was the younger boy, Thulo, who spoke up first.

"Telephone, you don't scare us! You don't deserve the mind stone and you will never get it," Thulo said. This was definitely not what the Demon King wanted to hear.

General Greymon hissed at Thulo, "Say our leader's name with respect. He is Lord Teninone. "

Thulo retorted, "He is unworthy of any title. In fact, he should be called the Brainless Gnome."

Teninone seethed. "Impudent kid. You don't know my power! Do you know what Teninone means? It means Ten-in-one! I have ten clones. We see, think, and do ten things at once—"

"And make ten times the mess", ten-year-old Pratham now added calmly. Then, turning to the soldiers, he said, "Evil always has an end, and your ruler's end is near. Leave him now and save yourselves."

Teninone was enraged but knew that if he killed the kids he might never find the mind stone. The mind stone was visible only to its owner and to whomever it was passed.

Ignoring the boys, he addressed Maya, "There is a prophecy that my death will neither be at the hand of demons, demigods, man, nor beast; neither by disease nor by one that is either young or old. I am practically immortal! As long as I live, I can do great things for the world with the mind stone. Tell me where the mind stone is and your family and friends will receive protection under my rule."

"If you promise not to misuse its power and also let humans and demons coexist peacefully, I will give it to you. I do not want a war where many innocent people—both humans and demons will die," Maya said. Teninone nodded his assent. With the mind stone, he might not need a war to become the ruler of the world.

Pratham and Thulo protested loudly, "You can't trust him! Don't give him the stone Maya!" But Maya had already started walking towards Teninone, a glowing crystal in her hand.

Teninone was ecstatic getting the stone from Maya. He tested his will on one soldier, willing him to stand on his head. It worked!

"Seer Shukra, you may take the kids back to Bhrigu. This was easier than I thought," laughed Teninone as he walked away with his prize.

Seer Shukra dropped the kids off. Bhrigu had a car waiting. It would take them to the hotel where Mom, Dad, and Peamon were staying.

On the ride to the hotel, Bhrigu asked, "So Maya, did you give Teninone the mind stone?"

Pratham and Thulo said at once, "Yes, she did! We tried to stop her, but she didn't listen."

"How did Teninone react?" asked Bhrigu.

"He was thrilled to get the mind stone. He tested out its power on one of his soldiers. He made the soldier do a headstand. For a moment, I thought I should freeze time and take the stone back. But as soon as Teninone held it, it became invisible again," said Matya.

"All that glitters isn't gold," said Bhrigu, mysteriously. "Anyway, Maya can explain her actions after dinner tonight. Until then, let's not bother her."

When they reached the hotel, they found that a table had been set up for their dinner. Mom, Dad, and Peamon were sitting at the table.

"Hurry up kids, we have delicious noodle soup for all of you," said Mom.

"I have a question. How much soup is in the bowl? Is it more than a cup of noodle soup? A bowl may be too much for me," said Thulo.

"Do you want to know the volume of a bowl, Thulo? For that, you need to know how to find the volume of a hemisphere. These bowls are hemispheres. I'll show you how to find their volumes," said Pratham as he began to draw on his phone:

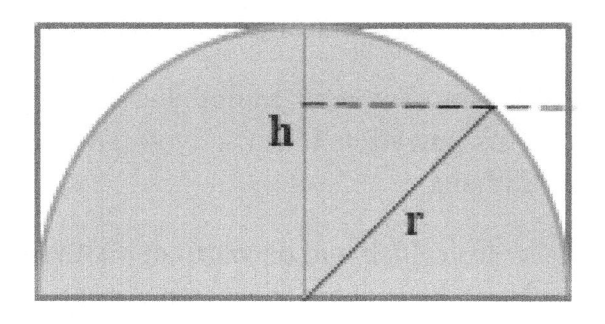

"I have drawn the cross-section of a hemisphere (green) placed within a cylinder (blue outline). The hemisphere's volume is the sum of the volumes of thin discs of decreasing radius as we go from the bottom to the top. At any given height, **h**, the area of the disc is $\sim 3 \times (r^2 - h^2) = 3 \times r^2 - 3 \times h^2$. If we stack discs of area $3 \times r^2$, what do we get? We get a cylinder with radius and height = r. And if we stack discs of area $3 \times h^2$, what do we get? We get a cone with radius and height = r! So the volume of a hemisphere is the difference of these two volumes: $\sim 3 \times r^3 - r^3$ or approximately $2 \times r^3$. Volume of a sphere is twice of this."

Volume of hemisphere $\sim 2 \times r^3$

"Wait a minute. How do you know the area of a disc is $\sim 3 \times (r^2 - h^2)$?" asked Thulo.

"You will learn about this later. Baudhayana wrote almost 3000 years ago, in 800 BCE, that the diagonal length produces a square equal to the sum of the squares of the vertical and horizontal lengths. Much later, Pythagoras re-discovered it. Look at the triangle with diagonal r. Its vertical length is h, and its horizontal length is the disc radius. Let's call it 'd'. Then $r^2 = h^2 + d^2$. That means the area of the disc $\sim 3 \times d^2$ or $3 \times (r^2 - h^2)$."

Thulo estimated the volume of the bowls and found it was not much bigger than the cups. Now that he was no longer worried, he began his dinner.

After dinner, the kids began chatting about the mind stone again.

"Did you really see into Teninone's mind and know for sure that he won't misuse its power? Is that why you gave him the mind stone?" asked Pratham.

"Oh, I clearly saw his selfish and deceitful mind. Even though he will try to avoid war, he is going to try and use it in any manner he feels necessary to realize his dream of ruling humanity," said Maya.

"Then why did you give it to him? That's just crazy!" said Thulo, who had become quite upset.

"Maya, please tell us the complete story. A girl as intelligent and caring as you must have had a very good reason for doing what you did," said Mom.

"When I was handed the mind stone, it revealed its mysteries to me. I learned that it is kind of like a powerful magnet. You know how you can magnetize pieces of iron with a powerful magnet? Similarly, the mind stone can transfer its power to certain crystals. The crystal can act like a very weak mind stone for some time; after that it loses its power. When Seer Bhrigu handed me the mind stone, he also handed me the crystals," said Maya.

"Why give him anything at all?" asked Peamon.

"I thought it would buy us time and he would leave us alone for a while," said Maya.

"Do you feel that was wise, Seer Bhrigu? When Teninone figures out he was tricked, he will want to exact his revenge on these kids," said Dad.

"Maya acted on her intuition and for the best. Only the future can tell how wise a particular action is. What seems most foolish today might turn out to be the best choice in the future, and vice-versa. The safest best is to act with noble intentions, for then God is on our side and can correct things as needed," said Bhrigu.

Practice Problem

A cone, a square pyramid (base is a square), and a hemisphere are all 6 inches wide. The cone and pyramid are 4 inches tall. All objects are open-ended. What are their volumes and surface areas? Which object has the largest volume? Which object has the smallest surface area?

Answer

First, let's find the volumes. Since widths are 6 inches, the cone and hemisphere have radius = 3 inches.

Cone volume ~ $r^2 \times h = 3^2 \times 4 = 36$ cubic inches.

Hemisphere volume ~ $2 \times r^3 = 2 \times 3^3 = 2 \times 27 = 54$ cubic inches.

Pyramid volume = $12 \times h = 12 \times 4 = 48$ cubic inches

To find the surface area of the cone and pyramid, we need to know the slant length, L. The height is 4 inches, and radius is 3 inches Using Baudhayana's Theorem, $L^2 = r^2 + h^2 = 3^2 + 4^2 = 9 + 16 = 25$. This means $L \times L = 25$. So $L = 5$.

Cone surface area ~ $3 \times r \times L = 3 \times 3 \times 5 = 45$ square inches.

Hemisphere surface area ~ $6 \times r^2 = 6 \times 3^2 = 6 \times 9 = 54$ square inches.

Pyramid surface area = Average perimeter × L = half of 6 × 4 × L = 12 × L = 12 × 5 = 60 square inches.

The hemisphere has the largest volume. The cone has the smallest surface area.

Chapter 9 The Tiger's Nest

Multiplication with different number systems

Dad did not seem to be consoled by Bhrigu's reply.

Bhrigu continued, "However, Maya did as I had hoped she would. I do need some time for the kids. They need to undergo rigorous training now."

"Training? For what?" asked Mom.

"Training to lead an army," said Bhrigu quietly. "As I said before, I have worked very hard to get you all here. I need help from these kids. Help to lead an army that will stop Teninone's ambitions."

"You will not take these kids to lead an army. They are too young. And they have nothing to do with Teninone or his ambitions," said Mom.

"I want to lead an army!" Thulo said. He thought it was like being the line-leader at school.

"Don't speak about things you know nothing about," said Mom.

"Don't show me angry eyes. I get scared," said Thulo.

"You are afraid of angry eyes, but want to lead an army," said Pratham as he shook his head.

Thulo gave his brother a shove, "I am not afraid of anyone!"

"I can understand a Mother's heart. You do not want any harm to come to the children. But what about the millions of others who will grow up to lead miserable lives working day and night like slaves in the world Teninone wants to establish?" asked Bhrigu.

"Why do you need these children? Why not anyone else? And again, why any children at all? Shouldn't this be a job for grown-ups?" asked Mom.

"They are the only ones who can learn to use special celestial weapons fast enough before the impending war. They will need to learn much to lead an army. Normally it would take years. But, they will learn it all in a month," said Bhrigu.

"How is that possible? It takes me some time to learn most things. Though I always get it all down by the end through patience, and sometimes with help," said Matya.

"Have you kids heard of Shambhala?" asked Bhrigu.

"I think I have," said Peamon. "Is it a mythical kingdom of eternal peace and joy? Where the people never age and are full of wisdom?"

"I think I've heard of it too," said Maya and Pratham simultaneously.

"Well it is no myth," said Bhrigu. "But we can't go there. If we do, we will most likely never return. Physical time stops there. But there are many dimensions that we need to go through before reaching Shambhala. And at each stage, while physical time slows down, mental time speeds up. In a few days, you will understand what it would normally take months to learn."

"Then why can't anyone go?" asked Thulo.

"To reach the higher dimensions, you need to have a certain level of purity of the heart. Children have the purest hearts. And your hearts are very special. The purity you have within expresses itself in different ways: bravery, compassion, love of truth, justice, and strong resolve," said Bhrigu.

"However, in that dimension, the denizens use a different number system more suited for measurements. Using it they advanced tremendously in the manufacture of both musical instruments and weapons. Long long ago they used to visit Earth quite regularly and were known as the Gandharvas. You will need to learn their number system to operate their weapons effectively," Bhrigu continued.

"What number system is that?" asked Pratham.

"They use a twelve digit number system called the dozenal system. It has two more digits than our ten digit decimal system," said Bhrigu.

"Wait. We count by twelves too, even though we use ten digits. Grocers sell eggs by the dozen; bakers sell donuts by the dozen; the carpenter uses a 12 inches foot ruler; and the jeweler and pharmacist use a 12 ounce pound measure. We also have 12 months in the year, and 12 hours for AM and PM. So why do we need a system with twelve digits when we can already count by twelves' just fine?" asked Matya.

"I think I can guess. It can make many measurements and calculations easier. The numbers 2, 3, 4, and 6 are all factors of 12. So divisibility rules become simpler. And, I guess multiplication tables become simpler too as there are more patterns to spot," said Pratham.

"Yes, your guess is accurate," said Bhrigu.

"How do we write the two extra digits?" asked Thulo.

"Ten can be written as X. And eleven can be written as E," said Bhrigu.

"So that means the multiplication table will look something like this," said Maya as she drew

1	2	3	4	5	6	7	8	9	X	E	10
2	4	6	8	X	10	12	14	16	18	1X	20
3	6	9	10	13	16	19	20	23	26	29	30
4	8	10	14	18	20	24	28	30	34	38	40
5	X	13	18	21	26	2E	34	39	42	47	50
6	10	16	20	26	30	36	40	46	50	56	60
7	12	19	24	2E	36	41	48	53	5X	65	70
8	14	20	28	34	40	48	54	60	68	74	80
9	16	23	30	39	46	53	60	69	76	83	90
X	18	26	34	42	50	5X	68	76	84	92	X0
E	1X	29	38	47	56	65	74	83	92	X1	E0
10	20	30	40	50	60	70	80	90	X0	E0	100

"And divisibility rules will become easier as follows," added Peamon as he drew:

Factor	Base 12 divisibility rule	Example Number	Explanation
2	Number ends in 0, 2, 4, 6, 8 or X	32	32 ends in 2.
3	Number ends in 0, 3, 6, or 9	76	76 ends in 6.
5	*Decimal sum of one's digit + 2 × ten's digit, ends in 0 or 5*	163	3 + 6 × 2 = 15, end in 5.
7	Sum of 3 × one's digit and rest of the number, is a multiple of 7	352	35 + 2 × 3 = 41, 4 + 3 × 1 = 7 (note all operations are in base 12).
E	Sum of digits is multiple of E	137	1 + 3 + 7 = E

But Mom wasn't listening to any of this. She was a feeling worried the kids would be away from her care.

"How long will they be away? Will they get proper meals? How will they reach these places?" asked Mom.

"We will be away for 3 days. We will need to walk up to the Tiger's Nest Temple and enter a secret portal there that will take us to the next dimension. An invisible Tiger guards the portal. The kids will need to answer his questions before he will grant them entry. However, I have faith in their wisdom," said Bhrigu.

"But what about their meals?" asked Mom.

"That will be attended to as well. You will have no complaint on that account," said Bhrigu.

"You said it would take a month for the kids to learn everything. But you also said you will be back in three days. I don't understand," said Dad.

"That's a good question. We can't remain in any of the higher dimensions for more than three days. Once the mind gets a taste of the knowledge and joy in these dimensions, it starts losing interest in coming back to this world. Staying in any dimension for more than three days will make it impossible for us to return to this world. We will spend 3 days every week there for the next four weeks," said Bhrigu.

"How do you know all this? If no one can return to say what happens on staying beyond three days in these dimensions, how do you know any of this?" asked Dad.

"Good question. A special class of beings can travel throughout all such dimensions without any limitation. They are the Time Lords – known also as Avatars in this world. It is from them that we know all this," said Bhrigu.

The next day, Bhrigu took the five kids to the Tiger's Nest Temple. Entering a secret passage within, they entered a round chamber. Once inside, the door vanished. There seemed to be no way back out.

In the empty room, they could feel a presence, and then they heard a low growl. "Welcome back Seer Bhrigu," said a deep voice that seemed to come from everywhere in the room.

"You are free to enter the portal, but your companions can not. You know the rules. They must answer my questions to enter the portal. But I am in a generous mood today. Since they have shown such eagerness to come, if they fail to answer correctly, they can remain forever here with me in the Tiger's Nest!" said the voice.

"Tiger, as you can see, these kids are brave. Your empty threat did not fluster them. I am old, but not senile. I have chosen these kids carefully. I know they can answer your questions. Please proceed," said Bhrigu.

A giant tiger materialized in the center of the room. It looked very fierce. The kids had a quiet confidence in themselves and did not feel afraid.

"I see some of you have the marks of the rainbow powers. Impressive. But that may not be sufficient to meet my challenge," said the Tiger.

The tiger walked up to Pratham and circled him slowly. Then he said, "You have the mark of bravery and unselfishness. Tell me then, boy, what must one fear?"

"Loss of character," Pratham replied.

The Tiger was surprised. How did the boy get the answer so quickly?

"That was a simple question. Now answer what must one hoard?" asked the Tiger.

"Good virtues like honor, courage, truth, compassion, optimism and patience," Pratham replied.

Peamon beamed at his friend's success. "So was that a simple question too, Mr. Tiger?" he asked.

The tiger felt annoyed and turned his attention to Peamon. "You do not seem to have any mark. What is your special quality I wonder? My questions are simple and yet you may not be a match for them. Here is my question to you. Doing what does all good virtues come to you naturally?" asked the Tiger.

"Treating thy neighbor – no matter who – as thyself," said Peamon. Pratham patted Peamon's back in appreciation of the answer.

The tiger stumbled back. Who were these kids and how were they answering his questions with such ease?

He turned his attention to Maya. Circling her slowly, he said, "You have the mark of knowledge. You can see into minds? Well, answer me this. What must one make an effort to overlook? And what must one make an effort to always see?"

"One must make an effort to overlook other's faults; and also make an effort to see the good qualities in others" replied Maya.

The tiger glanced at Bhrigu to check if he had been helping the kids in any manner. But Bhrigu was standing motionless in the room.

Now the Tiger circled Matya. "Little girl, I see you have the mark of Time. A patient person peers into eternity. You have no age any more, but you need not disguise yourself as a six year old. Here is my question for you – about what must one always be impatient?"

"One must always be impatient about purifying one's heart" replied Matya.

The Tiger looked like he had a bad taste in his mouth. "What trickery is this Bhrigu? Have you brought little kids to make a mockery of my challenge?"

"Please calm yourself Tiger. Your questions are excellent. But these kids are special too," said Bhrigu.

Now the Tiger tuned his attention to Thulo. If this little kid could answer his question too, then maybe it was time to find another job. The Tiger circled Thulo and said, "I see you have the mark of love. How can one know if it is true?"

"Love is like a triangle. It needs three points – there can be no fear in love, there can be no shop-keeping in love, and love must be for no other reason than itself," replied Thulo.

The tiger could not believe this. He would need to scare the little boy into answering incorrectly. "Very good. But here is my final challenge question to you. Can one love a beast?" asked the Tiger as he bared his teeth and put on his fiercest look, ready to pounce on Thulo. If any of the other kids dared to interfere, he would attack them – and see for sure if they were just smart alecks or real warriors.

To be continued ....

Made in the USA
Monee, IL
01 June 2020